# Blessed or Cursed?

The Message of Paul's letter to the Galatians

**Les Wheeldon**

Copyright © 2015 Les Wheeldon

All rights reserved.

ISBN-13: 978-1508636755

ISBN-10: 1508636753

ACKNOWLEDGMENTS

Many friends and Bible teachers have contributed to my understanding of the Bible and I am grateful to a long line of such people who have enriched and deepened my spiritual life.

For this book on Galatians special thanks go to my wife Vicki, and Jo Hawkins who contributed much both with ideas and patient, meticulous editing. My good friend Cyril Thomas sat with me for many enjoyable hours and offered much vital constructive advice on the form and content of the book. Heartfelt thanks go to all these who have encouraged me and contributed in such significant ways.

Les Wheeldon

## *CONTENTS*

The story of Reggie Law and Joshua Grace .................................................................. 4

    The apostle's burden ................................................................................. 7

    There is only one gospel ........................................................................... 7

    When did Paul write to the Galatians? ........................................................ 10

    What is the central message of Galatians? ................................................. 12

    The structure of the epistle ...................................................................... 13

Chapter 1

    The apostle's conversion ......................................................................... 20

Chapter 2

    At Jerusalem – confirmation from the apostles ........................................... 29

    At Antioch – conflict with the apostles. ..................................................... 32

    The Ten Commandments and Sabbath Day observance. ............................. 40

Chapter 3

    Blessing and curse .................................................................................. 52

    True Abrahamic blessing: to be justified by faith ........................................ 57

    The law is our tutor to bring us to God ..................................................... 62

Chapter 4

    From slavery to sonship ........................................................................... 64

    Fears for the Church ............................................................................... 67

    Which covenant do we live under: old or new? ........................................... 70

Chapter 5

    The choice: a life of love or a life of sin ..................................................... 75

    Life in the flesh ....................................................................................... 77

    Life in the Spirit ...................................................................................... 81

    3. The presence of God is the atmosphere of growth. ................................. 85

Chapter 6

    The apostle's passion .............................................................................. 97

STUDY GUIDE A: GENERAL QUESTIONS:..................................................101

STUDY GUIDE B: CHAPTER BY CHAPTER................................................104

All scripture quotations, unless otherwise indicated, are taken from the New King James Version®. Copyright © 1982 by Thomas Nelson, Inc.

Used by permission. All rights reserved.

# THE STORY OF REGGIE LAW AND JOSHUA GRACE

When Christiana first met Reggie Law, she was so impressed with his high standards and absolute integrity that her admiration of him grew and grew. One cannot talk of love at first sight because there was far too much sternness in his approach to their relationship. Everything was weighed by its ultimate usefulness but she was drawn to his devotion to do what was right, and so after a short engagement they were married in church (with appropriate expense - but measured by the need to save money for the missions' fund).

Her first realisation that married life was not going to be easy came during their honeymoon. He was up at dawn like clockwork and woke her not with a cup of tea but with a rather heavy book entitled, *"Plumbing the depths of religious devotion."* She had felt a twinge of guilt because she had really wanted to sleep in for an hour or two but realised that he was right, and she should be up and praying for the day's activities.

However, things turned a little sour when they settled into their daily routine. He instructed her that he wanted dinner punctually at 6pm, and whenever it was served a minute late, she was left with no doubts about his displeasure. After dinner he would wander round the house and point out areas where she had obviously failed to keep up the required standards, such as the dust that had settled on the door lintel, or the occasional spider's web that had appeared in some hidden corner. Life became hard and burdensome.

It was after they had been married for 10 years that she received the shocking phone call that he had collapsed at work and been rushed into hospital. When she got there, the doctor met her with a grim but compassionate expression.  Reggie Law had suffered a massive heart attack and had died.

Christiana was genuinely sad, but felt a little guilty at a tiny wave of relief.  It was during the funeral that she caught herself smiling, and even had to hide her face in a hanky to prevent anyone seeing the joy that welled up.....

Two years later she met Joshua Grace.  He was kind and attentive to her. She had certainly not been expecting that she would ever meet anyone as good and upright as Reggie had been. Josh was, if anything, of an even higher standard than Reggie had been, but you would never have known it from his relaxed and happy demeanour.  His smile was infectious and his presence made it so easy for her to laugh again.  They were married one year after their first meeting and he swept her off her feet, taking her on a fantastic cruise for their honeymoon. He read to her amazing stories of bravery and adventure by people whose courage, kindness and faith she had never imagined possible.  He seemed to know about many people who had been so bad and whose lives had been so lost in darkness, but there was always some miracle that came along to turn things round.

At home Josh never complained about anything and, if there was any dust or cobwebs to be cleaned, he got on with the job and did it himself.  He didn't mind doing chores like cleaning the toilets.  He even regularly washed the rubbish bins.  He bought her flowers and gifts so often it was embarrassing. Christiana found herself singing at the top of her voice while she did the housework, and worked longer and harder than she had ever done before.  She began to understand what it meant to want to live forever because she never wanted her life with Josh to end.

*"Therefore my brethren, you also have become dead to the law through the body of Christ, that you may be married to another."* Romans 7:4.

"Run, John run,
The Law commands,
But gives me neither feet nor hands,
Tis better news the Gospel brings,
It bids me fly and gives me wings."

John Bunyan,
"The Doctrine of the Law and Grace Unfolded" 1659.

## *The apostle's burden*

It is rare to read a book that deeply changes our life. But these six little chapters of Paul's letter to the Galatians have precisely that power; to transform us and our whole approach to Christ and the Christian life. God Himself was speaking to the Christians in Galatia and beyond them to Christians everywhere. This short letter can open up a world of love, joy and peace in the power of the Holy Spirit.

The letter to the Galatians was not written to convert unbelievers, although it does contain many truths applicable to all people. This letter is a declaration of the foundation of Christian living. It is a vital message for all Christians to understand.

## *There is only one gospel*

Today it is hard to imagine a time without at least two churches in every village, not to speak of dozens of churches in many cities. Moreover even within the four walls of each church may be found several interpretations of scripture on foundational doctrines such as evidence of the Spirit's indwelling, not to mention views about the second coming.

On the first day of the church's existence there was joy, gladness and unity of faith in the apostles' teaching. They were all of one heart and rejoiced in that unity. The preaching of the apostles was not based on opinion polls or surveys to find out what the believers felt should be preached, no more than Jesus had leaned on the mood of the crowds for guidance. The new-born church spoke with clarity about the person of Jesus, His divine nature, the centrality of His cross, the reality of His resurrection and the wonder of His gift of grace that Jesus lives in His people through the Holy Spirit. In fact these truths breathe through all the writings of the New Testament. Yet within a short period of around 20 years we read in Acts 15:5 of doctrinal division:

*"But some of the sect of the Pharisees who believed rose up, saying, "It is necessary to circumcise them, and to command them to keep the Law of Moses.""* Acts 15:5

The fact that the church had reached its 20th birthday without division was in itself remarkable. They had found the resources in the person of the Holy Spirit to heal doctrinal division and to reaffirm central truths.

Peter declared in Acts 15 that salvation for Jew and Gentile was through grace; which opened the door for the purifying of hearts through faith, by the gift of the Holy Spirit (Acts 15:8-11). Peter, in a few words, summed up this specific foundation of apostolic teaching which was being threatened by this Pharisaical sect. Peter spoke with the authority of experience and was backed up forcefully by the testimony of Paul and Barnabas. The words of these great men were then confirmed by the sober James, expounding the scriptures with these vital words:

*"And with this the words of the prophets agree, just as it is written."* Acts 15:15

This was a defining moment in church history. The New Testament church affirmed that there is but one gospel by which we can be saved. If we lose sight of this gospel then there is no message of eternal salvation among God's people any more than in a book club, or a political party.

Paul, in Galatians 1:8, makes a startling proclamation. He curses anyone who preaches another gospel than the one which he himself preached. This is very important since it reveals the truth that there is incredible danger when preachers do not declare the truth of God as it is in Christ. There are many reasons why preachers change the gospel: some have never experienced the saving transforming grace of God, others have become cynical, while others have embraced an emphasis that subtly and unconsciously changes the gospel. Paul says they are to be cursed whoever they are, and even includes the possibility of himself in this, showing that it was not about a conflict of personalities but the greater ground of eternal truth by which we will all one day be judged.

> *"But even if we, or an angel from heaven, preach any other gospel to you than what we have preached to you, let him be accursed."* Gal 1:8

Paul obviously believed that the gospel was not his own invention, nor was it something to be tampered with or adjusted. It was a message from God to be held in great reverence and godly fear, most of all by those who preach it.

This puts all other matters into context. It is far too easy to blame humanists and atheists for the problems of our society. In Paul's day there was fierce persecution from pagan governments and immoral cultures - yet Paul does not waste time bewailing the waywardness of the world. He returns to the great centre of all things. The gospel of salvation is the special gift of God to His people. Only as the church lives in the full gift of the grace of God does it have relevance and power in the society in which it exists.

We must seek to be modern and relevant for our generation. However, this must never be achieved by changing the message. God's people must abide in the authority of God, in the wonder of the gospel, and in the power of the Holy Spirit. Spiritual decline in a nation should not be traced back to the door of the humanists; it should only be traced back to the tragic neglect of biblical truth among God's people, leading to a loss of spiritual power and dynamism. Galatians is relevant to all generations as it seeks to bring believers back to the key foundations of life in Christ.

## *When did Paul write to the Galatians?*

Paul was converted around 32 AD, three years after the resurrection which is believed to have been around 29 AD. He spent three years in Damascus and then paid a short visit to the apostles in Jerusalem (Acts 9:26-30; Galatians 1:18). Paul then lived in Tarsus until Barnabas persuaded him to join the work in Antioch around 45 AD (Acts 11:25). He then visited Jerusalem with Barnabas 14 years after his conversion around 46 AD (Acts 11:30; Galatians 2:1). Paul then departed on his first short missionary journey around 47-8 AD which included his visit to four cities of Galatia: Antioch (in Pisidia), Iconium, Lystra and Derbe (Acts 13 and 14).

In Antioch and Iconium some Jews and many Gentiles received his message, but he was rejected by a forceful and determined opposition (Acts 14:5). Paul fled to Lystra where God enabled him to do a remarkable miracle and a lame man was healed (Acts 14:9). This miracle stunned the whole community and at first the people believed Paul was a god. But after a few days some antagonists arrived from Antioch and Iconium who turned the city against Paul. The crowds of people turned into a violent, angry mob and Paul was stoned.

Stoning is an ugly method of execution still practised in some countries and is even sanctioned by some governments today. Paul would have borne dreadful physical scars for the rest of his life and yet it was at this moment that he had a remarkable experience of God's power. The crowd dragged Paul out of the city and left him for dead. Some have wondered if he did in fact die and was raised from the dead. Paul himself may not have been sure but it is certain that he experienced an astonishing miracle. The believers stood around him when suddenly he rose to his feet in full health. His recovery was instant and dramatic. His body was totally restored to life and vitality, his heart filled with vigorous courage. Completely undaunted by the events, he rose up and preached again in the very cities that had persecuted him (Acts 14:20-21).

Some have speculated that Paul may have had an out of body vision of heaven through this near-death experience. Paul tells of such an experience in 2 Corinthians 12:2 and it is possible that he is describing what happened at this moment. However 2 Corinthians was written at the latest in 57 AD, which would mean that his out of the body experience was in 43 AD some four years before his visit to Galatia in AD 47 when he was still living in Tarsus.

Remarkably, only a short time after these events, the churches in Galatia were being troubled by "Judaizers" who were persuading Gentile converts of the need to get circumcised and keep the law of Moses in order to be saved. This opposition probably occurred within months of Paul's visit which caused him to marvel how quickly the believers had been corrupted from their faith (Galatians 1:6).

Paul then, wrote this letter probably from Antioch around 48-49 AD just before the council in Jerusalem in Acts 15. If that council had already taken place then Paul would almost certainly have mentioned it. The meeting described in Galatians 2 bears no resemblance to the large and tense gathering described in Acts 15 which must have taken place weeks after this letter was written.

## *What is the central message of Galatians?*

The overall theme of this letter is the simplicity of the gospel of salvation. We are told in Acts 15:1 that Judean visitors came down to Antioch and started teaching that a believer must be circumcised according to the Law of Moses in order to be saved. On receiving news that this doctrine had already been preached in Galatia, Paul wrote quickly to refute this false gospel and to remind the Galatians of the real basis of their salvation.

What then was the apostle's burden? His message can be summed up by four key statements:

*1. We are accepted by God through faith in His Son. This acceptance is total and cannot be improved upon by any rite such as circumcision or any human effort.*

*2. The Christian life is a life of surrender to the Spirit of God.*

*3. The Holy Spirit produces in us the kind of life that God desires. The Christian life is likened to a seed growing into a mature fruit-bearing plant. All the seed needs is good soil, sunlight and water. Christ is the seed, our believing hearts are the soil, the Holy Spirit is the water and the sunlight is God's love. If we maintain these conditions, God will cultivate a Christ-like character in us.*

*4. Even the smallest amount of human striving (the flesh at its best) can undermine the activity of the Spirit which is through faith. This can then cause our lives to descend into empty religion, ruined by sinful behaviour (the flesh at its worst). We can never earn favour with God through works but are to direct our energies into enjoying His presence and embracing the cross as a doorway to life in the Spirit.*

## *The structure of the epistle:*

| Gal 1:1-5 | Paul's introduction | His apostleship came from God not man |
|---|---|---|
| Gal 1:6-10 | Paul's purpose in writing | To combat the corruption of the Galatian believers from the simplicity of the gospel |
| Gal 1:11-24 | Paul's testimony | His salvation from the emptiness of man-centred religion |
| Gal 2 | Paul's authority | The gospel he preached and his relationship with the other apostles. The means by which a person is saved. |
| Gal 3 | A blessing and a curse | The cursed emptiness of self effort compared with the blessedness of a life of faith in the power of the Spirit |
| Gal 4 | Man's infancy | Life under the law is like infancy compared with the glory of the new covenant that makes us sons of God |
| Gal 5 | The choice | Spirit or flesh, a life of love or a life of sin. |
| Gal 6:1-10 | The freedom to serve | Practical implications of living by grace. |
| Gal 6:11-18 | Paul's passionate appeal | Paul is consumed with the cross and its effect on his life |

# CHAPTER 1

### *Paul's greetings: Galatians 1:1-5*

> *Paul, an apostle (not from men nor through man, but through Jesus Christ and God the Father who raised Him from the dead), 2 and all the brethren who are with me, 3 Grace to you and peace from God the Father and our Lord Jesus Christ, 4 who gave Himself for our sins, that He might deliver us from this present evil age, according to the will of our God and Father, 5 to whom be glory forever and ever. Amen.*

These opening verses are believed to be the first recorded lines that ever came from the apostle's pen. His brief greetings include his first reference to the resurrection (1:1) and the cross (1:4).

These are the foundations of all that Paul preached and they are his consistent theme through all his writings. His message is simple: Christ, who is God in human form, died for the sins of the world and rose again from the dead. This simple fact is the centre of history, and the transforming focus of God's message to mankind in the gospel.

Paul also here makes his claim that his authority is not from man but has a divine origin and stamp of approval (1:1). This is to be further explained later in the chapter and it is a key part of his message to the church in Galatia.

It is also here that Paul introduces his distinctive greeting that is in every one of his thirteen letters: his desire for grace and peace to be the experience of his readers (1:3).

## *Paul's purpose in writing: Galatians 1:6-10*

> *⁶ I marvel that you are turning away so soon from Him who called you in the grace of Christ, to a different gospel, ⁷ which is not another; but there are some who trouble you and want to pervert the gospel of Christ. ⁸ But even if we, or an angel from heaven, preach any other gospel to you than what we have preached to you, let him be accursed. ⁹ As we have said before, so now I say again, if anyone preaches any other gospel to you than what you have received, let him be accursed. ¹⁰ For do I now persuade men, or God? Or do I seek to please men? For if I still pleased men, I would not be a bondservant of Christ.*

In all of Paul's other letters he introduces himself and says something positive about the people he is writing to. Paul even does this in his first letter to the Corinthians where he probably had to think hard to find something good to say. However here in his letter to the Galatians Paul skips these opening niceties and goes straight to the problem facing the Galatian churches.

In v 6 he would have startled them with his directness. He makes the challenging assertion that this fledgling church was turning away from Christ. They would have been shocked at the thought that they were deserting Christ for another gospel. He boldly states that a curse should be on anyone who preaches another way to be saved. The gospel is more important than the preacher and he includes himself by saying *"even if we"* preach or change this gospel, let us/them be accursed. Paul was not simply using strong language when he said this; he was showing the inevitable results of such a path. What form would this curse take? God alone can know how He deals with each individual, but the curse must be, at the very least, the loss of the life-giving, healing presence of God. Spiritual darkness and heaviness would steal over such believers, making their efforts fruitless and destroying hope and joy in their own hearts. To preach another gospel is a path of great foolishness for it is to make an enemy of God.

Paul's mention of angels is arresting. Fascination with angels is quite easy to understand. From time to time we hear and read about angelic messages and visitations - but these must be tested. The words of an angel must never be set above the Word of God as an angelic message may not be from God; it could be from Satan who would gladly dilute the power of the gospel. The Bible says that there are deceiving spirits and that Satan himself is transformed into an angel of light (2 Cor. 11:14).

Paul sets the gospel itself above the preacher, the messengers, ministers and apostles, and even angels. Paul has this awareness, which comes through his writings, that he is handling something far greater than himself. Preachers should give their listeners a sense of awe at the greatness and majesty of their subject. They must convey that they are not themselves the answer; Paul had an extraordinarily powerful ministry but in Romans 1:16 he says that *"the gospel is the power of God"* not his own ministry. The power is in the gospel to make Christians into overcomers. The victorious

Christian life is not a myth like the pot of gold at the end of the rainbow. There is power in the Holy Spirit to overcome our sin and even our self-centredness, and enable us to have a life centred on Christ.

Since the first century and down to our present day there has been a temptation to pollute Christian doctrine with humanist philosophy. This looks on the positive side of human nature; it seeks to highlight the good things that God sees in us and that we can contribute to His kingdom. Side issues become central such as good causes or political considerations. Money becomes important as a means of doing God's work, and slowly and subtly the power of the gospel is lost, as the emphasis shifts from God to man. We still long for revival but feel that the answer apparently lies with us. If we will only put more effort in, even pray more earnestly, have bigger prayer rallies; maybe then God will reward us. The result is strain not faith. More prayer is good so long as we do not subtly transfer our faith in God, to faith in our own zeal.

The word "Judaizers" comes from a Greek verb used in Galatians 2:14 meaning "to live according to Jewish customs." Judaizers, refers to that group of Jewish believers who made Moses' law and especially circumcision into a condition for salvation and membership of the church (Acts 15:1). It was such a small ceremony and yet it came to symbolise trust in their own ability to do something for God, to earn acceptance with God. The corruption that Paul saw in their actions was that they led to a belief that men and women are the great deciders, and masters of their own fate. At best the Judaizers sought to honour God by a rigid observance of Old Covenant practice. The subtle danger of such legalism lies in that it is always appealing to do more, to strive harder, to go to greater lengths and show greater sacrifice.

There is no such appeal in the preaching of Christ, nor was there a hint in His devotion to the Father that He was straining to do more for God as His life unfolded. The life of Christ was at rest in the midst of intense activity for His Father. It is that centre of rest into which we are to be introduced.

> *In the 19th century there were two well-known preachers in London, one named Parker and the other was Spurgeon. A visitor to London wrote in his journal "I went to hear Parker in the morning and came away thinking - what a great preacher! I went to hear Spurgeon in the evening and came away thinking – what a great God!"*

Do we leave the impression that the answer lies with human effort, or that there is a great God who has the answer?

God has to disturb the faith we have in our own ability because only Christ has the power to save. The problems in society cannot be solved by politicians, atheists or humanists; they can only be solved by the gospel. The danger lies in the corruption of Christianity. Paul is saying: Get the teaching right. Right teaching produces right churches. Right churches can be an influence for good in society. Wrong doctrine is like dry rot and it can quickly infect the whole church. Dry rot in a house spreads rapidly and can bring it down unless discovered and treated early. Leviticus describes God's instructions if a house is leprous; if the infection cannot be removed (Lev 14:41) then the house must be destroyed (Lev 14:45).

The light of the cross brings a dreadful awareness that all my efforts have bolstered my pride and my sense of achievement. They have taken my soul further from God rather than into the nearness of fellowship that I so longed for. God does not build on our efforts or on the capable, the rich, the strong or the clever. God in Christ has crucified our old nature. He has crucified our selfishness, along with all our passions and desires, and worldly ambitions. In the place of this self-centred life, He has planted Christ. We live in Him and rest in His presence.

This is the exchanged life that Paul saw as the great key to our human condition. Christ had done this for him and could do it for anyone who would enter in by simple faith. In Christ we can live a life for God without guilt, strain or self-effort and without producing a sense of failure. The gospel is Christ Himself living in us producing the same poise and calm that can be seen in Christ. It is not a mixture of Christ and human effort; it is I in Christ and Christ in me.

## The Apostle's conversion

## The foundation of Paul's ministry: Galatians 1:11-24

> [11] But I make known to you, brethren, that the gospel which was preached by me is not according to man. [12] For I neither received it from man, nor was I taught it, but it came through the revelation of Jesus Christ. [13] For you have heard of my former conduct in Judaism, how I persecuted the church of God beyond measure and tried to destroy it. [14] And I advanced in Judaism beyond many of my contemporaries in my own nation, being more exceedingly zealous for the traditions of my fathers.
>
> [15] But when it pleased God, who separated me from my mother's womb and called me through His grace, [16] to reveal His Son in me, that I might preach Him among the Gentiles, I did not immediately confer with flesh and blood, [17] nor did I go up to Jerusalem to those who were apostles before me; but I went to Arabia, and returned again to Damascus.
>
> [18] Then after three years I went up to Jerusalem to see Peter, and remained with him fifteen days. [19] But I saw none of the other apostles except James, the Lord's brother. [20] (Now concerning the things which I write to you, indeed, before God, I do not lie.)
>
> [21] Afterward I went into the regions of Syria and Cilicia. [22] And I was unknown by face to the churches of Judea which were in Christ. [23] But they were hearing only, "He who formerly persecuted us now preaches the faith which he once tried to destroy." [24] And they glorified God in me.

## Pastor, are you saved?

> *Recently, when travelling in Romania, I was introduced to a family in the small town of Ocna Mures. There were three generations in that little house, and such warmth and love from son Mihail, mama and grandma. Ninety year- old Grandma, gripped my hand, fixed me with her eye and asked: "Are you a Christian?"*
>
> *Mama interrupted: "He's a pastor Grandma, he's a pastor!" "Yes, yes, but is he a Christian?" persisted Grandma.*

Even pastors, missionaries and apostles must have a personal testimony of salvation and of life with God. It is easy to forget that Judas joined the other disciples in their ministry as an apostle with power and miraculous signs. He did this while not being truly repentant; he continued stealing from the common purse (John 12:6). This fact alone should cause us to ponder the reality and truth of what men preach and the outworking of this in their lives. Signs and wonders are part of God's promise to His people, but we must not be led astray from the foundations of the gospel which are the truths set out in Galatians.

Many testimonies begin with words like "I was a drug addict" or "I was a criminal" or even "I was a terrorist." We love these dramatic testimonies and sometimes use them as star attractions. There is of course something very heart warming when someone declares how they were saved from their personal life of hell. God's power is glorified and we are moved by the love and the mercy of God. However testimony should not be mainly about our former life, but about our new life.

While always ready to give his testimony to those who did not know Christ, the majority of Paul's preaching and teaching concerned the life he had entered into, not the life he had left behind.

> *Evangelist Keith Kelly, as a young Christian, was asked to give his testimony in a tent crusade in Denistoun, Glasgow in 1984. He was the last one in a group of testimonies. There were former street fighters who gave an electrifying account of their former life of violence before coming to Christ – one told of throwing someone through a plate glass window! There were several who spoke vividly of the darkness of battling with drug addiction till Christ saved them. When it came to Keith's turn he stood up and said how he had been a stamp collector in his former life! He was an ordinary guy...but he was not saved. He needed Jesus to change him just as much as the others.*

Saul was not a morally depraved man who had a problem with adultery or drunkenness. His sin was religious. He had almost certainly been brought up in a strict environment and had even attended the best Bible school of the day. He had embarked upon a religious career - serving God with all the zeal he could muster. However Saul did not know what God was like and when Christ met him on the Damascus road, He exposed Saul's spiritual blindness with that searching question:

*"Saul, Saul, why are you persecuting me?"* Acts 9:4

Jesus did not speak to Saul in anger but addressed him with compassion and understanding of his confused religious state:

*"I am Jesus whom you are persecuting. It is hard for you to kick against the goads."* Acts 9:5

Christ looked on this passionately religious man and summed up his existence by telling him how hard it was for him to fight against His love. Saul's state, although deeply religious, was nonetheless sinful. Saul was doing what he thought was best but getting nowhere. It was the awareness of his own background that now inspired the apostle to resist at all costs any sign of the church drifting back into the very condition from which he personally had been saved.

In this moment of encounter with Christ, all his religious striving became pointless and foolish. Why? Because he had seen Jesus. A brief glimpse of Jesus can change us forever. What did he see? There was brightness sufficient to blind him physically but there was also compassion in those tender words of pity. There was no anger, bitterness or frustration; rather there was Christ's majestic authority that caused Saul to cry out "Lord!" for the first time. This is the essence of conversion - we must all have a personal encounter with Jesus.

The impact of such an encounter with Christ will convince the deepest sceptic. Saul had rejected the deity of Christ until this moment and yet now accepted Him as Lord and Master without a word of argument. This is why Paul declares in Galatians 1:12 that he had not been taught the gospel. He had not imbibed it in a lecture hall. He had understood it in a moment of revelation. This fact can humble even the most powerful minds, as here God is revealing that spiritual understanding does not depend on our power of intellect but on our attitude of heart. When our hearts are wrong, our minds can never fathom spiritual matters but, when our hearts are right, understanding floods in.

Pride can exclude us from God's presence but the humble broken heart passes straight in. God does not communicate just through the reasoning faculties. If He did, then the cleverest Christians would be the most spiritual - which is far from the truth. God communicates through the revelation given to the heart by the Holy Spirit. This does not deny the importance of intellect; it rather demonstrates that there is a deeper realm. Understanding is a matter of the heart as much as of the brain.

> *"The heart has its reasons, which reason does not know. It is the heart which experiences God, and not the reason. This, then, is faith: God felt by the heart, not by the reason."* Blaise Pascal, Pensees.

Saul's experience on the Damascus Road exposed the emptiness of all his striving; in that moment he let go of his ambitions and his attempts to please God through his own efforts.

In Galatians chapter one, Paul's testimony is not just about what he was saved **from**, but what he was saved **to**. He claims that his former sinful life was one of hypocrisy and religious bigotry. In his letter to the Galatians, Paul is showing how "sin" is not just the wrong things we do; it can also be human zeal for God which produces spiritual pride and arrogance. We need salvation from dead and arrogant religion in whatever form it takes.

Saul had been turned around by a glimpse of Jesus to a life immersed **in** Him. Christ had been revealed to him just as when the old fashioned camera shutter opens and the image is imprinted on the film inside. Saul prayed in wonder for three days, just as Jesus in the tomb awaited the Resurrection. What did Saul see as he waited? He saw that he was justified - he could not have explained it to anyone, but he knew in a flash that Jesus had accepted him totally as His own. No part of the Christian life can be separated from Jesus. All is in and through

His wonderful person. Saul could see that something had satisfied God more fully and totally than all the generations of religious struggle to please God. There was warmth, tenderness, and forgiveness in the face of Jesus.

> *The conversion experience of C.S. Lewis:*
>
> *"You must picture me alone in that room at Magdalen, night after night, feeling, whenever my mind lifted even for a second from my work, the steady, unrelenting approach of Him whom I so earnestly desired not to meet. That which I greatly feared had at last come upon me. In the Trinity Term of 1929 I gave in, and admitted that God was God, and knelt and prayed: perhaps, that night, the most dejected and reluctant convert in all England"*
>
> *(Surprised By Joy, C.S. Lewis, chapter 14).*

Whether you are brought to your knees by a blinding light or alone in your room as "the most reluctant convert in all England" – true conversion is the result of an encounter with the living Christ pouring light into our hearts.

Paul sums up his testimony in 2 Cor. 4:6:

> *"For it is the God who commanded light to shine out of darkness, who has shone in our hearts to give the light of the knowledge of the glory of God in the face of Jesus Christ."*

So Saul did not wait in despondency, though he had good reason to be depressed; after all, he was blind. His pride had been struck a death blow, but this was not a cruel death, but one which satisfied deep longings to be free from guilt and to be right with God - he had come home. We can perhaps imagine Saul praying in calm wonder for three days and on the third day Ananias entered his room declaring:

> *"Brother Saul, the Lord Jesus, who appeared to you on the road as you came, has sent me that you may receive your sight, and be filled with the Holy Spirit."* Acts 9:17

The words were new: "be filled with the Holy Spirit." Ambition and selfish striving had been struck a mortal blow three days earlier and his mind was becoming clearer than ever before. He was ready. He felt the hands of Ananias, heard his voice as he began to pray, and suddenly light poured in from all directions. His physical eyes were opened and inwardly the Holy Spirit flooded his whole being, revealing God's wondrous plan of salvation in him:

> *"It pleased God to reveal His Son IN ME."* (1:16)

> *"I have been crucified with Christ; it is no longer I who live, but Christ lives IN ME."* (2:20)

The Glorious One who had been revealed on the road was now being revealed in Saul's heart. In the depths of his own being, there now shone the wonderful person he had met with and seen three days earlier. The effect was indescribable. Truth about God and salvation poured into him faster than he could assimilate it. The whole experience was utterly mind-blowing; Saul realised that this was a whole new order of life.

Look at Jesus - look long and hard. Search the gospels, read about Him and then direct your heart to Him in prayer. Saul had to be led by the hand, and so must we. All human searching for truth through philosophy and intelligence is ultimately worthless - we must be helped by God to find the truth. Philosophy has only value in exploring the human condition but it has no value in answering the quest of the soul for God. Philosophy differs fundamentally from Christianity in that each philosopher sets out to invent and define God; while Christianity is the personal discovery of the God who reveals Himself.

If you hid a coin in a field 20 kilometres away and then told a blind man to find it on his own, you have an idea of the powerlessness of the human mind to find God. If the invisible God did not want us to find Him we would seek in vain. But He does want us to find Him and He will lead the seeking soul. When Saul met with Jesus, he began to pray, reaching out in his Spirit for God.

Salvation is radical. Human beings have no hand in it: it is an act of God. The converted Saul, (now Paul) was specially chosen to receive the revelation of all that salvation is and so was led out into the Arabian desert, to spend long months in communion with God, as God revealed the wonder of what had happened on the Damascus Road.

Paul was saved from the form of religion into the power of a relationship with Christ. God had His man, who was to stand in the gap and prevent the corruption of the gospel in the first century. Without this man, the whole of the New Testament church might have been swept away by the force of the waves of corrupt doctrine. The battle lines were forming and sooner or later the war would begin.

What were these revelations which Paul must have received during those days of waiting on God? Three great themes run through all his writings:

1. The revelation of the awesome majesty and supremacy of Jesus Christ as Messiah, Almighty God in human form.

2. The awful revelation of a life without Christ and the realisation of the emptiness of every human being separated from Him. Peter had seen the greatness of Christ and was the first to confess Him as Messiah, but when Peter became the first to deny Him, he faced the stark reality of what he was really capable of. Without Christ we are nothing, and the church can easily decline into a state as full of jealousy and pride, as any group of human beings.

3. The revelation that "I am in Christ and that Christ is in me" and that through His indwelling presence, I can be holy, spiritual, prayerful and full of love.

# CHAPTER 2

## *At Jerusalem - confirmation from the apostles*
## *Galatians 2:1-10*

*¹ Then after fourteen years I went up again to Jerusalem with Barnabas, and also took Titus with me. ² And I went up by revelation, and communicated to them that gospel which I preach among the Gentiles, but privately to those who were of reputation, lest by any means I might run, or had run, in vain.*

*³ Yet not even Titus who was with me, being a Greek, was compelled to be circumcised. ⁴ And this occurred because of false brethren secretly brought in (who came in by stealth to spy out our liberty which we have in Christ Jesus, that they might bring us into bondage), ⁵ to whom we did not yield submission even for an hour, that the truth of the gospel might continue with you.*

*⁶ But from those who seemed to be something—whatever they were, it makes no difference to me; God shows personal favouritism to no man—for those who seemed to be something added nothing to me. ⁷ But on the contrary, when they saw that the gospel for the uncircumcised had been committed to me, as the gospel for the circumcised was to Peter ⁸ (for He who worked effectively in Peter for the apostleship to the circumcised also worked effectively in me toward the Gentiles),*

> *9 and when James, Cephas, and John, who seemed to be pillars, perceived the grace that had been given to me, they gave me and Barnabas the right hand of fellowship, that we should go to the Gentiles and they to the circumcised. 10 They desired only that we should remember the poor, the very thing which I also was eager to do.*

In Galatians chapter two we have to understand the background of what had happened. Paul is describing his relationship with the original apostles, especially with Peter and John, and also with James, (the brother of the Lord who was the leader of the church in Jerusalem). Everyone sensed the great authority which lay in these three men.

Sooner or later after his conversion, Paul had to meet with the apostles. His first meeting had been very brief (described in Acts 9:27-30). After Barnabas had brought Paul to Antioch (Acts 11:25-26) Paul's stature and influence grew and a more formal meeting was necessary (which is probably his visit to Jerusalem described in Acts 11:30-12:25). He had to share with them the revelations he had received, in order to confirm the truth of the things that had been revealed to him.

Paul had received tremendous revelation, and yet he says:

> *"And I went up by revelation, and communicated to them that gospel which I preach among the Gentiles, but privately to those who were of reputation, lest by any means I should run, or had run, in vain." (2:2)*

There is tremendous humility in this statement, a profound realisation that as wonderful as revelation may be, it must be confirmed in fellowship with other believers and in harmony with the writings of the original apostles. Paul went privately to meet the apostles in order to submit to them the essence of his preaching.

His description of the apostles is filled with meaning:

> *"But from those who seemed to be something—whatever they were, it makes no difference to me; God shows personal favouritism to no man—for those who seemed to be something added nothing to me." (2:6)*

In attempting to imagine that meeting, we can picture the initial hesitation and then the warmth that quickly flowed as Paul told them of how he had received revelations and wrought miracles. He in his turn would have basked in the wonder of firsthand accounts of the person of Jesus - all confirming that this was the very same person he had since met through the Spirit. As they shared, Paul would have expressed things about the cross and the church, and the apostles would have looked at each other in wonder, realising that this man had gone on further in the things of God than they had. Yet all that he was saying was in line with the things that they too had received.

What joy there must have been that day, in the realisation that the work of the Lord would not decline with the passing of the original apostles. God was demonstrating that He could raise up witnesses to the gospel in any age.

The apostles then gave to Paul and Barnabas the right hand of fellowship, their confirmation and seal on the life and teachings of Paul. He himself was grateful and yet, as his words suggest, he had not been overawed by the meeting, but rather there was possibly a slight hint of disappointment that they had not had more to say to him: *"for those who seemed to be something added nothing to me" (2:6)*. He seems to have felt that apostles should have gone a whole lot deeper than they had. Even at that early stage, he may have sensed that they were not as liberated from the power of man-centred religion as they should have been.

The conclusion of the meeting in Jerusalem was clear. Paul was a bona-fide minister of the gospel as much as all the apostles. But the harmony between Christians from Jewish and Gentile backgrounds was soon to face its most importance test of all - in the Gentile city of Antioch.

## At Antioch - conflict with the apostles
## Galatians 2:11-13

> [11] *Now when Peter had come to Antioch, I withstood him to his face, because he was to be blamed;* [12] *for before certain men came from James, he would eat with the Gentiles; but when they came, he withdrew and separated himself, fearing those who were of the circumcision.* [13] *And the rest of the Jews also played the hypocrite with him, so that even Barnabas was carried away with their hypocrisy.*

The setting was perfect. The work at Antioch was fresh and new, and there were Christians from both Jewish and Gentile backgrounds. God had apparently made both one, having *"broken down the middle wall of separation:"* (Ephesians 2:14), but then came the visiting preacher - the apostle Peter. This visit must have taken place in the period when Paul was settled at Antioch either just before his first missionary journey or immediately after it, but at least before Acts 15. At first Peter seems to have rejoiced and entered into the new-found equality of Jew and Gentile Christians at Antioch. He had already seen the need for this liberty when he had preached the gospel at Caesarea to the household of Cornelius. He had entered the house of a Gentile and had fellowshipped with them, and this he continued to do while at Antioch.

Then along came some brothers sent by James, from Jerusalem. What they said is not recorded and we are left to guess. We know that the effect of their words on Peter and Barnabas was to make them withdraw from eating with the Gentiles. Peter had once more caved-in under pressure as he had done on the night in which Jesus was betrayed and he had denied the Lord three times.

On the rooftop at Joppa, Peter had received a special vision that the Gentiles were not to be called unclean (Acts 10). This revelation had included an instruction to break the dietary laws of Moses and eat pork! (Pork was not specifically mentioned, just the general phrase "unclean" foods). But now in Antioch Peter was denying the Lord's revelation to him.

This whole event teaches us how easily we can yield to pressure and shift our ground on things that were once so obvious. By the grace of God 'the cock was about to crow' but this time - by the voice of the apostle Paul. This may make us smile, but it should alert us to the need for ministers who are willing to wake up believers to the dangers of compromise. Such ministry will help to prevent doctrinal drift that can cause us in the end to deny the Lord. The cock crows in the early morning waking up the sleepers. This is the ministry that Peter needed now.

## *Galatians 2:14-21*

*¹⁴ But when I saw that they were not straightforward about the truth of the gospel, I said to Peter before them all, "If you, being a Jew, live in the manner of Gentiles and not as the Jews, why do you compel Gentiles to live as Jews? ¹⁵ We who are Jews by nature, and not sinners of the Gentiles, ¹⁶ knowing that a man is not justified by the works of the law but by faith in Jesus Christ, even we have believed in Christ Jesus, that we might be justified by faith in Christ and not by the works of the law; for by the works of the law no flesh shall be justified.*

*¹⁷ "But if, while we seek to be justified by Christ, we ourselves also are found sinners, is Christ therefore a minister of sin? Certainly not! ¹⁸ For if I build again those things which I destroyed, I make myself a transgressor. ¹⁹ For I through the law died to the law that I might live to God. ²⁰ I have been crucified with Christ; it is no longer I who live, but Christ lives in me; and the life which I now live in the flesh I live by faith in the Son of God, who loved me and gave Himself for me. ²¹ I do not set aside the grace of God; for if righteousness comes through the law, then Christ died in vain."*

The pressure on Peter had come from that ancient city Jerusalem where James was the prominent leader. Surrounded by the symbols of Old Covenant religion, the church there had begun to mix the old with the new. This leads inevitably to confusion and difficulties in the churches which Peter was now being forced to wrestle with again. This error struck at the heart of the gospel, which is what James in Jerusalem and Peter in Antioch failed to see. Ancient Jerusalem with its altar, its temple, its symbols and history was not to be seen as the fountain of life and truth. The 'New Jerusalem' with a New Covenant, had been brought in, and old and new must not be mixed. This meant in practical terms, that each individual Christian had to renounce religious man-centred effort as useless in the service of God, and much more importantly, as useless in the attainment of salvation. Salvation could not be earned by works but by grace alone.

Paul, in opposing Peter publicly, was setting a standard for the church of the New Testament and for the church in every generation. Paul was not seeking personal conflict with Peter; he was bringing Peter back to the truth by which both men had been saved and which both had earlier agreed upon. Paul`s statement to Peter was heavy with apostolic authority which Peter could not oppose.

The harmony found in Paul's first visit to Jerusalem was now facing its greatest test. Perhaps the conflict had been postponed by the fact that they had agreed to work in different areas: Paul among the Gentiles and the others among the Jews. Of course this could only defer the conflict since these two worlds could not ultimately be kept apart. Peter, James and John had obviously been fighting shy of some of the issues, perhaps through the pressure of the large numbers of believers in Jerusalem who were still zealous for the law (Acts 21:20). Was it still needful to keep the law in order to be saved? If not then why should even Jews continue to keep it? The answer is of course that they did not need to keep the law to be saved. Jews might keep the law for other reasons, such as respect for the conscience of other Jews but not in order to obtain salvation.

Paul's attitude to his fellow apostles is arresting. It is worth spending time here, noticing some important things we can learn from Paul about our attitudes towards those in authority in the church. It is easy to understand Peter's fallibility. After all he sank in the waves on the Sea of Galilee through unbelief and he denied the Lord three times. But even John should not be set on a pedestal. He was the beloved apostle whom Jesus loved, who wrote the gospel, who leaned on Jesus' shoulder... but he was not infallible. Catholics have made the saints into something divine as our mediators, and have elevated their leader into the infallible status of supreme Pontiff. Protestants have often attacked these practices, while forgetting that the danger of elevating people does not only lie in the Roman Catholic institution: it lies in the human heart.

We can so easily exalt ministers into infallible popes - transferring the authority of the message to the messenger,

> *As one Protestant said to a Catholic: "It is easy for you - you only have one pope... while we have hundreds."*

rushing to hear what they say as if their opinions are the Word of God. This is not to deny the possibility of spiritual depth and power, since all of these apostles had attained true stature in Christ. However Paul himself was aware of his fallibility and thanked God for the infirmities that kept him dependent on grace (2 Corinthians 12:9-10). Ministers can so easily be raised above what is healthy either for God's people or for themselves.

What is true spiritual maturity? Three marks of true greatness can be found in this chapter:

1. Honouring others. When James, Peter and John listened to Paul, they recognised in him the authority of God. They did not think of him as inferior to them because had not walked with Jesus as one of His disciples. It is a sign of greatness to be able to listen to another ministry and discern God's voice.

2. Courage. Paul's lion-like greatness is shown by his fearlessness in standing alone; he opposed them publicly to safeguard the purity of the gospel. He was not defending himself; he was willing to be nothing and be rejected by the church for defending the gospel of God.

3. Able to receive correction. The third sign of greatness that is implicit in this chapter is in the reaction of Peter. There is no record of how he reacted to such a public rebuke, but we can infer that he received correction meekly with an ability to admit he was wrong. This impression is supported by the warmth of Peter's later commendation of Paul in 2 Peter 3:15: "Our beloved brother Paul, according to the wisdom given to him." Peter was humble and not afraid to "lose face" over this. Paul had this same attitude of willingness to lose all in order to gain Christ (Philippians 3:8). In reality when we lose our self importance, we actually gain. Jesus said "Whoever saves his life will lose it." Success alone is not a sign of spiritual greatness for by success we are tempted to be proud and to reject correction.

> *"He is no fool who gives what he cannot keep to gain what he cannot lose," Jim Elliott.*

How humbling it is that God often has to raise up a man who is not in the centre of things in the churches and yet who is much more in the centre of things that God is doing. Tyndale, Luther, Wesley, Fox, Spurgeon, to name but a few, had to plough a very lonely furrow in order to fight for the truths that they had discovered in their simple reading of the scripture. So many pioneers are outcasts, and it is to be wondered if in

Jerusalem, Paul ever had the total acceptance that was due to him, as a minister of God. He might have been considered a little threatening. At any rate, we are left to wonder why the apostles considered it right that Paul should go to the Gentiles and they to the Jews. After all, Jesus had given to Peter and John the divine commission to go into all the world and preach the gospel, which later on they were to fulfil. However at this moment they were apparently still wrestling with their Jewishness and the demands of the law.

At this point, it must be made clear that the issue at stake was the ritual law not the moral law of the Old Covenant. The two can easily be confused, and there are areas where they overlap. The moral law is contained in the Ten Commandments, which contain no ritual, and which is perfectly fulfilled through the power of the Spirit in the New Covenant. The ritual law is contained in all the ordinances of the Old Covenant, including animal sacrifices, and all the feasts. These are all now obsolete by the fact that they were prophetic and temporary, and have found their perfect fulfilment in the Messiah: the Christ.

> *"So let no one judge you in food or in drink, or regarding a festival or a new moon or Sabbaths, which are a shadow of things to come, but the substance is of Christ,"* Colossians 2:16-17.

One of the great lessons of this chapter is that it shows us the danger of losing our liberty and the power of the gospel, through legalism and dead religion. Paul introduces the subject of circumcision and also dietary laws. There were 613 laws in the Law of Moses to do with rituals and diet. If we, under the New Covenant, start insisting on keeping one or two of the Old Covenant laws, the Bible says we must keep ALL of them. Paul says later in Galatians 5:3; "I testify again to every man who becomes circumcised that he is a debtor to keep the whole law." They would have to bring in animal sacrifice, never eat pork and certain seafood, as well as observe the Sabbath day (Saturday not Sunday). Paul is pointing out that if we insist on keeping one or more of these mosaic laws and start saying that people have to do this or else they are not saved, then we have changed the basis of salvation.

Once we elevate one bit of law, it becomes the tip of the iceberg. Even in the Old Testament, it was never intended for people to think that they could be right through religiously keeping the law. They were also saved by grace alone. Even Moses was not good enough to enter the Promised Land, he needed grace. All have sinned and fallen short of the glory of God. Nobody is good enough by their own efforts or righteousness. This is wonderful news for anyone who feels a failure or too bad to be saved. We are not saved by our degree of holiness or by knowing the Bible well enough. The preaching of legalism results in people feeling that they have to try harder; the more you try – the more God will accept you, the more God will move. God says no! It is by faith, through grace; which is how you start, how you go on and then how you finish.

Both Jew and Gentile are to look on the cross as the fulfilment of prophecy. Once a year, the High Priest in the Old Testament had access to the Holy of Holies on the Day of Atonement. The coming of the Holy Spirit and the creation of the church (with no partitions of race or gender) make the Day of Atonement obsolete, since God's people now have permanent unlimited access to God whose house is His people not the temple in Jerusalem. The New Testament is the fulfilment of the hopes of God's ancient people the Jews. There was only ever one who could keep the law, and that was Jesus. His righteousness is imputed to us when we put our trust in Him.

## *The Ten Commandments & Sabbath Day observance*

Where then do the moral and ritual law overlap? The most obvious area is in the observance of the Sabbath day. This by its very nature involves action of some kind. "Thou shalt not kill" is fulfilled by non action, containing not a shred of ritual. But observance of a day of rest contains positive action - obedience. This can easily spill over into ritual observance of rules and regulations, without realising the spiritual significance of the day of rest. Similarly to spiritualise everything can result in neglect of God's practical command, resulting in disobedience.

How is the Sabbath to be interpreted under the New Covenant? This can only be understood by reference to the first Sabbath when God Himself rested after creating the world. God was not tired. His rest was the rest of love fulfilled and a goal attained. Naomi in Ruth 3:18 gives a vital insight into this rest when she said of Boaz: "*... the man will not rest until he has concluded the matter this day.*" Boaz was not tired but simply restless till he had won Ruth as his bride. Similarly Jesus Christ was restless till he had paid the price for our salvation and could cry out from the cross *"It is finished!"* (John 19:30). This cry echoes Genesis 2:1 *"Thus the heavens and the earth and all the host of them were finished."* God rested after the creation of man for he had attained his goal. When sin entered the human race God could not rest till He had attained the goal of our salvation, reconciling the world to Himself.

What is the Sabbath rest for the Christian? Firstly it is not about a day of the week, but about a spiritual principle. We must enter into rest of heart through the forgiveness of sins. The main cause of restlessness is guilt, and this will have an effect on our whole personality, physical and spiritual. Stress raises blood pressure, causes muscles to be tense, produces aches, pains and stomach ulcers. Through faith and the cleansing power of Jesus' blood, we may all enter into peace with God and find a dimension to life in which we can find increasing freedom from stress. The Christian life is not a life-long striving to get right with God. It begins with the amazing realisation that I am right with God through the finished work of Christ on Calvary. The Christian life begins not with "do" but with "done."

Secondly we must take practical steps to maintain this rest of soul. The world is littered with Christian ministers who have suffered from burnout. In fact, in so many prayer letters you can hear the desire to justify one's ministry by being as busy as possible. Each must decide what this means in practice but there is divine wisdom in observing one day a week for rest, quiet, worship and meditation. Without a Sabbath there is a danger that God will be crowded out of our busy lives. God does not disregard our physical and mental need of simple rest.

Thirdly we must learn to roll our burdens on the Lord and live without worry or fear. There is a deeper rest for those who wait on God. God is able to take all stress from our souls and give us a child-like trust and confidence that He is in control and more than able to turn even the worst situation to good.

Lastly, we must not legalistically impose our own views on others. Some keep their Sunday special, others insist it is the Saturday, while others see every day the same. Paul warns us not to be legalistic and divisive in the way we view the Sabbath day. The gospel is the power of God to salvation, and in the preaching of the gospel, the significance of the Sabbath has nothing to do with what people have been doing on Sunday. It has rather to do with the fact that men and women have made no room for God in their lives, let alone in their weekly timetable. There are millions who do not work on Sunday but who will do anything but think of God. They have rested their bodies but they have forgotten God. Being free from law means that each Christian is at liberty to understand why and how God commands us to rest. This means much more than observing Sunday as a day of rest but rather has implications for the way we live as a whole.

> *Hudson Taylor's Sabbath Rest.*
>
> *On one occasion, George Nicol was with Hudson Taylor when a pile of letters brought news of dangers and problems facing a number of missionaries. Taylor leaned against his desk to read them and began to whistle "Jesus I am resting, resting, in the joy of what Thou art, I am finding out the fullness of Thy loving heart." (Taylor's favourite hymn).*
>
> *"How can you whistle, when our friends are in such danger?" Nicol asked.*
>
> *"Suppose I were to sit down here and burden my heart with all these things; that wouldn't help them, and it would unfit me for the work I have to do. I have just to roll the burden on the Lord."*
>
> *(from J. Hudson Taylor, a Man in Christ by R. Steer; p.265).*

## Paul confronts Peter

Paul's great declaration to Peter in the second half of chapter two is not a logical argument leading from one point to another. Rather, it is summary of five great foundations of salvation. Several of these had respect to an immediate crisis, while others rank among the greatest statements of New Testament truth.

### 1. Jews have been relieved of the obligation to keep the ritual law.

*"If you, being a Jew, live in the manner of the Gentiles, and not as the Jews, why do you compel Gentiles to lives as Jews? We who are Jews by nature and not sinners of the Gentiles, knowing that a man is not justified by the works of the law but by faith in Jesus Christ and not by the works of the law; for by the works of the law no flesh shall be justified." (2:14-16)*

Jews may now live freely among the Gentiles with a good conscience, eating formerly forbidden meats and with no need to celebrate the feasts. He says that he and Peter are Jews by nature. He implies that through the force of their culture and upbringing, Jewishness had passed into their subconscious mind, and was part of them as an underlying second nature. It was easy for them to live as Jews, but not at all easy for the Gentiles to adapt to Jewish ways. Peter and Paul had been led to cast off this nature, and to live as Gentiles with the Gentiles. The unity of the church does not lie in Old Testament law. Today a missionary to unconverted Jews would be as sensitive to Jewish tradition as Paul was, when he had Timothy circumcised in Acts 16:3. But this would be the wisdom of God for love's sake, not the foundation of salvation.

If Christians are to be truly a witness to the world, we must be liberated from trusting in outward forms and live as Christ among the men and women of the world.

> *Pause for a moment, and reflect on what this may mean for us. Is there anything unhelpful which has become second nature, which would be as hard to cast off as the issues facing Peter and James?*
>
> *Recently I spoke at an evangelistic Bible study. Afterwards, during the question and answer time, a man asked why I had not made the sign of the cross before praying and opening the meeting!*
>
> *I explained that this was a tradition which was not laid down in scripture, but then I realised that this man had been brought up in the Greek Orthodox religion where it was almost unthinkable for him to approach God without employing this sign.*
>
> *But have we formed our own liturgy? Do our meetings fall into a set form or pattern that cannot be changed?*

## 2. Acceptance with God is by His Grace alone.

Justification by faith means that each one is given right standing with God as a gift. This is through the forgiveness of sins, and yet it introduces us to life without any need to try and please God by our own efforts. Not only is my past sinful life forgiven, but I am received as sinless in His sight. This is not only for a moment, so that I might try and be better, rather this acceptance is the foundation of my new life. It liberates me to receive the Holy Spirit. It gives me the grounds for daily fellowship with God. It is the foundation of spiritual life. By this gift all need for religious striving and tension is swept aside. I can breathe a sigh of relief and rest at last. I am right with God through something Christ has done, not through my works.

## 3. This gift is for the repentant.

Repentance is described in two ways in Galatians. Firstly in chapter 2:18 where he speaks of "those things which I destroyed;" and then secondly in chapter 5:24 as the act of "crucifying the flesh with its passions and desires." Destruction speaks of the radical forsaking of sinful habits and ways. Crucifying the flesh speaks of the total abhorrence and rejection of a former way of life.

Those who believe they can continue sinning because they are justified by faith are deluded. Without repentance no man can be justified and if we return to sin we imperil our right standing with God. Repentance is not making myself perfect, nor is it a promise to try better next time. Repentance is all to do with the way we look at sin. The unrepentant person looks at sin as a cherished friend, like a miser who has to pay his taxes or else go to prison. He loves his money and parts with it unwillingly, as if it were part of himself. He caresses his money before finally handing it over, always waiting till the last moment before parting with it. This is outward but not inward repentance. The truly repentant build a metaphorical bonfire with their money and dance at the sound of the flames which signal their deliverance.

The truly repentant person sees the evil he has loved as a viper, and is amazed and grateful that he has not perished earlier. Now he casts the viper from him, crushing its head with shouts of joy and relief. Such a man knows that he cannot overcome sin in his own strength and rejoices when he finds the way of escape.

When Zacchaeus repented of his life of fraud, he received Christ joyfully, and gave back four times what he had obtained by deceit, and gave half his money to the poor! He had repented of his sin, received Christ, and Jesus declared: "Today salvation has come to this house!" (Luke 19:1-10).

## 4. *The work of God in my heart is through faith.*

The remarkable emphasis in Paul's declaration is that it is not only **my** faith that saves me, but the faith of Christ Himself. This is hidden in most translations and Galatians 2:16 and 2:20 offer the interpretation "faith **in** Jesus Christ" whereas the Greek text can be translated "the faith **of** Jesus Christ". This is puzzling and bewildering at first, until I suddenly remember how shaky and unreliable my own attempts to believe are. How grateful we must be that our salvation does not rest entirely on our own faith but on the faith of the Son of God Himself.

This can be seen at the resurrection of Lazarus. Jesus raised Lazarus partly in response to the faith of Martha! But He did not raise Lazarus by Martha's faith! She could not imagine what Jesus was about to do, but she trusted Him knowing that He was the answer to the situation:

> "Now *Martha said to Jesus, Lord, if you had been here, my brother would not have died. But even now I know that, whatever You ask of God, God will give You." (John 11:21-22)*

God Himself lives and works by faith. This is a fact that may easily be overlooked because God's faith is in His own word and power. There are three supreme examples of God's faith in action:

- When He created the world His words spoken by faith brought the physical universe into existence (Hebrews 11:3). Faith is the atmosphere He breathes, and is to become our way of life also.

- When Jesus comes back, He will raise the dead, and those who are alive on the earth, will meet Him in the air. (1 Thess. 4: 16,17) All these things can take place in our lives, because we believe in Jesus. Yet none of them will take place by our personal level of faith, but through the faith of the Son of God. He believes that He can raise the dead, and I believe in Him.

- Similarly Jesus believes that He can present me faultless, sinless, perfect and full of love before the throne of God, and I believe in Him. He believed as He died that His blood could wash me clean and make me fit to receive the Holy Spirit, and as I trust in Him, He through His own faith does the work. The miracle of new birth is far above what we can ask or think, and it is marvellous and right that it should be so. My faith is simply the hand lifted to Jesus, but it is the strong arm of God that lifts me!

> *His Faith or mine?*
>
> *Imagine a man lost out at sea. He is cold and very weak as he swims towards land, struggling to keep his head above water. A man on the cliff top spots him and calls for a rescue helicopter. Within 15 minutes, the helicopter is hovering above the man. The rescue team lets down a rope and instructs the man just to hold tight and cling to the rope, so that they can lift him out of the sea, up over the cliffs and rocks. They assure him that in fifteen minutes he will be safe.*
>
> *But the man has no strength, and his fingers are weak and the rope slippery. He wants to be saved, but he is too exhausted. Then a rescuer is lowered down on a harness, who instructs him to just reach up. The man raises his hands, and suddenly feels the iron grip of the rescuer.*
>
> *The man is lifted to safety, not by his own strength but by the skill and strength of his rescuer, who will not let him go.*

## 5. *The baptism with the Holy Spirit is an experience of the cross.*

One of the greatest statements that Paul ever made is in Galatians 2:20:

> *"I have been crucified with Christ; it is no longer I who live, but Christ lives in me; and the life which I now live in the flesh I live by faith in the Son of God, who loved me and gave Himself for me."*

This is his description of the baptism with the Holy Spirit, which is a phrase first used by John the Baptist, and then by Jesus. John the Baptist taught that water baptism was itself a picture of the greater baptism that the Messiah would give. It is remarkable that both in Galatians and Romans the phrase "baptism with the Holy Spirit" is completely absent. This does not mean that Paul does not talk about it, but rather that he refers to this great work by what it is in spiritual reality: an experience of the cross.

Baptism with the Spirit is an exchange of life for life, my sinful life for His pure life. We are brought into union with God Himself. There is no dependence there on what human beings can achieve, and Jesus, who is the root of all righteousness, is now at our disposal. A person can believe in Christ and through the power of the Holy Spirit simply rest in the glory of Christ within. It is no wonder that this life is described as joy unspeakable and full of glory.

The wonder of this is that all that Christ accomplished on the cross is made available to me. I can have a direct and real experience of the cross. No one suffers to atone for their own sin, yet to us is given the power and victory of the cross over sin. Christ identified with me in my sinful state, so now I can be identified with Christ in all His glory. Christ Himself prophesied this identification:

> *"... with the baptism that I am baptized with you will be baptized" (Mark 10:39)*

Baptism by immersion in water, and rising out of it, is a picture of Christ's death and Resurrection. Jesus was Himself baptised declaring his intention to be identified with sin on the cross. Jesus was prophesying His immersion into death, His rising again, and the Holy Spirit descending in response to His sacrifice. Now I am to identify with His death by faith, exchanging old life for new, by receiving the baptism with the Holy Spirit.

Being crucified with Christ, means that the believer has a cross in his or her heart - not cruel nails and a crown of thorns, but the instinct of self-emptying - of esteeming others - of taking the lower seat - of washing disciples' feet. No-one can ever hope to fulfil this royal law unless there is a mighty urge inside to do so. No-one can love grudgingly.

The miracle of the cross is that by it, I am made one with God which is the true miracle of the baptism with the Spirit. We must never lose sight of it or be deflected from it. We were made one with God by the death of Jesus and the gift of the Holy Spirit. This should revolutionise our whole thinking about ourselves and God. He is in us – and we have been empowered by the presence of the uncreated God in our hearts.

*John Sung wrote that if God anointed carnal men with the Holy Spirit, the result would be a monster!*

*"God does not confer His power on those who are full of "self"; it would help the "self" to mutate into Frankenstein if He does that!"*

*John Sung, The Diary Once Lost, p 171.*

# CHAPTER 3

### *Blessing and curse*
### *Galatians 3:1-14*

> *¹ O foolish Galatians! Who has bewitched you that you should not obey the truth, before whose eyes Jesus Christ was clearly portrayed among you as crucified? ² This only I want to learn from you: Did you receive the Spirit by the works of the law, or by the hearing of faith? ³ Are you so foolish? Having begun in the Spirit, are you now being made perfect by the flesh? ⁴ Have you suffered so many things in vain—if indeed it was in vain?*
>
> *⁵ Therefore He who supplies the Spirit to you and works miracles among you, does He do it by the works of the law, or by the hearing of faith?— ⁶ just as Abraham "believed God, and it was accounted to him for righteousness." ⁷ Therefore know that only those who are of faith are sons of Abraham. ⁸ And the Scripture, foreseeing that God would justify the Gentiles by faith, preached the gospel to Abraham beforehand, saying, "In you all the nations shall be blessed." ⁹ So then those who are of faith are blessed with believing Abraham.*
>
> *¹⁰ For as many as are of the works of the law are under the curse; for it is written, "Cursed is everyone who does not continue in all things which are written in the book of*

*the law, to do them." ¹¹ But that no one is justified by the law in the sight of God is evident, for "the just shall live by faith." ¹² Yet the law is not of faith, but "the man who does them shall live by them."*

*¹³ Christ has redeemed us from the curse of the law, having become a curse for us (for it is written, "Cursed is everyone who hangs on a tree"), ¹⁴ that the blessing of Abraham might come upon the Gentiles in Christ Jesus, that we might receive the promise of the Spirit through faith.*

In Galatians chapter three, Paul begins with the remark that Christ had been clearly portrayed as crucified among the Galatians (3:1). Some have speculated on Paul's powers of imagination and his theatrical abilities to make this possible. Nothing can be further from the truth. Paul did not present Christ through the use of natural gifts, but through the revelation of the Holy Spirit:

*"And my speech and my preaching were not with persuasive words of men's wisdom, but in demonstration of the Spirit and of power." (I Cor. 2:4)*

Through the preaching of Paul, the Galatians, like the Corinthians had seen the cross with their inward eyes. The result of this had been that Christ had ministered to them justification and then the power of the Holy Spirit. They had had a clear spiritual beginning. Galatians 3:3 refers to this beginning in the Spirit. How wonderful it is to have received the truth of God from an experienced minister. They were brought to the beginning of God's work in their heart through a clear baptism in the Spirit.

Many people do not have this privilege. Many hear the gospel preached by men like Apollos, who only know the baptism of John (Acts 19:25). This is a great tragedy, and by this error, many are forced to try to live New Testament Christianity without the power of Spirit baptism. The result is that many try to explain the scriptures in a way which discounts the powerful moving of the Spirit today, some even saying that the age of spiritual gifts is passed.

Some explain the power of the Spirit as a being who is present, while not being clearly felt. They also say that the presence of the Spirit is a doctrinal position rather than a conscious experience. At this point it is right to ask how a person would ever notice the Holy Spirit leaving their life if they had never noticed Him come into their life. This is a serious issue, since we are speaking of this blood-bought gift of the Saviour Himself, not an optional extra. It is because hearts are comforted into accepting something less than God's will, that many live without power over sin, the world, self and the devil.

A person is saved from the moment they trust in Christ. The baptism with the Holy Spirit is not a condition of salvation, it is a grace gift. Nevertheless a person only begins his fully equipped Christian life at the moment he receives the baptism with the Holy Spirit. He may begin his journey to this point many days even years before this, and he may be delayed through ignorance (as in the case of the Ephesian disciples in Acts. 19). Nevertheless it is God's clear will that believers be consciously immersed into the Spirit.

Paul's lament in Galatians chapter three is that they had not continued trusting in God's grace to grow as Christians. Just as the Baptism with the Holy Spirit is a gift, so also spiritual growth comes through the working of that Spirit. The Galatian believers had begun to set aside grace and to trust in their own efforts to take them further. This had one result; they began to experience all the curse of empty religion.

God is not asking us to do more and more for Him, He is simply asking us to continue in the same attitude of faith which we knew when we received the gift of the Holy Spirit. The great word in this chapter is "the curse." Few in the west are aware of the demonic curses that plague heathen cultures. Yet even in countries such as England, there are witches and evil men who practice witchcraft by putting a curse on someone. These things are all too familiar to those who live in Africa, where many are in constant terror of evil. Yet Paul says that there is a cursed state that is experienced by those who seek to serve God in their own strength!

> *"For as many as are of the works of the law are under the curse; for it is written, "Cursed is everyone who does not continue in all things which are written in the book of the law, to do them." (3:10)*

This curse is not some evil power working to cause illness and disaster. Rather it takes the form of heaviness, spiritual dullness, lack of zeal and love. It produces a sense of pride and superiority, and yet at the same time opens the door to shameful passions that rise up in the heart, contradicting the cherished ideals of the mind. Romans chapter seven is often interpreted in a gloomy manner to mean that a Christian will never be free from the struggle against inward sin. Hope grows dim, and the expectation of a long hard road through life settles on the heart. Sadness is the mark of the life, not joy and victory. Without repentance such a state of heart may become a way of life. However, Paul finishes Romans chapter seven by saying:

> "O wretched man that I am! Who will rescue me from this body of death? Thanks be to God through Jesus Christ our Lord!" (Romans 7:24, 25)

This is the very truth that Paul declares in Galatians 3: 13:

> "Christ has redeemed us from the curse of the law, having become a curse for us (for it is written, "Cursed is everyone who hangs on a tree")." (3:13)

Christ was identified with this cursed legalistic state as He hung on the cross. He crushed it under His foot. He erased it from the hearts of men and women by the power of His own life. He took the curse fully onto and into Himself; thereby destroying it. This is the mystery of the cross. God can destroy sinners and cities and worlds through fire and flood, but to destroy sin in the human heart required the power of God's own being. This is a mystery, and yet is the centre of all our faith, that Christ was made sin and a curse as He absorbed the awfulness of the human condition into Himself, thereby destroying it. It is by the miracle of identification and by this alone that we ourselves can be baptised, absorbed and immersed into the holiness and the love of God. As God was identified with me for my redemption, so too I must be identified with Christ. Each must receive the gift of baptismal identification with Christ.

> "But Jesus said to them, You do not know what you ask. Are you able to drink the cup that I drink, and be baptized with the baptism that I am baptized with? They said to him, "We are able." So Jesus said to them, "You will indeed drink the cup that I drink; and with the baptism that I am baptized with you will be baptized." (Mark 10:38 - 39)

These words of the Lord are a prophecy of the personal application of the cross to each individual by means of baptism with the Holy Spirit. It is by the power of this union with Christ that the Law finally becomes obsolete.

The Law is a tutor says Paul, to grant us some means of relating to God. But the Law is inappropriate when union with Christ has taken place. It is as if a couple were to get married and employed a solicitor to live with them to make communication between them easier! The need for Law implies a spiritual void in our hearts. But Christ came to meet this very need through baptismal union with Himself:

> *"For as many of you as were baptized into Christ have put on Christ." (3:27)*

This is not referring merely to water baptism, since water baptism itself is a metaphor of baptism with the Spirit into the death and Resurrection of Christ.

## *True Abrahamic Blessings.*
## *Galatians 3:14-29*

> *14 that the blessing of Abraham might come upon the Gentiles in Christ Jesus, that we might receive the promise of the Spirit through faith.*

> *15 Brethren, I speak in the manner of men: Though it is only a man's covenant, yet if it is confirmed, no one annuls or adds to it. 16 Now to Abraham and his Seed were the promises made. He does not say, "And to seeds," as of many, but as of one, "And to your Seed," who is Christ. 17 And this I say, that the law, which was four hundred and thirty years later, cannot annul the*

*covenant that was confirmed before by God in Christ, that it should make the promise of no effect. 18 For if the inheritance is of the law, it is no longer of promise; but God gave it to Abraham by promise.*

*19 What purpose then does the law serve? It was added because of transgressions, till the Seed should come to whom the promise was made; and it was appointed through angels by the hand of a mediator. 20 Now a mediator does not mediate for one only, but God is one.*

*21 Is the law then against the promises of God? Certainly not! For if there had been a law given which could have given life, truly righteousness would have been by the law. 22 But the Scripture has confined all under sin, that the promise by faith in Jesus Christ might be given to those who believe. 23 But before faith came, we were kept under guard by the law, kept for the faith which would afterward be revealed. 24 Therefore the law was our tutor to bring us to Christ, that we might be justified by faith. 25 But after faith has come, we are no longer under a tutor.*

*26 For you are all sons of God through faith in Christ Jesus. 27 For as many of you as were baptized into Christ have put on Christ. 28 There is neither Jew nor Greek, there is neither slave nor free, there is neither male nor female; for you are all one in Christ Jesus. 29 And if you are Christ's, then you are Abraham's seed, and heirs according to the promise.*

Paul first describes the blessing of Abraham as the consciousness of being justified by faith (Galatians 3:6; 3:24). This is the affirmation that when we trust in Christ, we have fulfilled all the requirements of God for salvation. God counts us not merely forgiven, but positively righteous and possessing all the virtues of His Son. No sin can ever be held against us, because Christ has paid for all our sin, and has suffered in our place the full penalty of God's Holy Law. This has removed forever the grounds by which Satan could accuse us. Abraham knew this blessing, and looked forward to the cross. The Old Testament sacrifices pointed to the cross, and all believers from Seth, through Noah, Moses, Samuel, Isaiah right through to John Baptist were accepted through faith, not by works.

Paul then describes the blessing of Abraham as the gift of the Holy Spirit (3:14). On rare occasions one hears the Holy Spirit spoken of as a threat. It is possible to heap condemnation on believers because they are not full of the Holy Spirit. This has the effect of increasing the barrier between the believer and the Holy Spirit. No one has the right to receive Him. Fortunately for all of us, His job is to take unworthy sinners and make them worthy by the blood of His Son, Jesus.

Imagine a father at Christmas time calling his children to receive their Christmas presents. He first reminds them of all the wrong things they have done, and then reproves them for their laziness and lack of diligence in the home. He makes them kneel and beg forgiveness before he hands over the gifts! Such a scene is horrific to any loving parent, and it is contrary to the heart of God. Jesus said: "Do not fear little flock, for it is your Father's good pleasure to give you the Kingdom." (Luke 12:32) Jesus emphasises in Luke 11:13 the greatness of God's desires to give the Holy Spirit, much more than an earthly father desires to give good gifts to his children.

Abraham and all the Old Testament believers received justification by faith: *"And he believed in the LORD and He counted it to him for righteousness"* (Genesis 15:6). But Old

Testament believers did not receive the baptism of the Holy Spirit:

> *"These all died in faith, not having received the promises, but having seen them afar off were assured of them, embraced them and confessed that they were strangers and pilgrims on the earth." (Hebrews 11:13)*

> *"And all these, having obtained a good testimony through faith, did not receive the promise." (Hebrews 11:39).*

This is the crucial difference between the Old and New Testaments, and is the reason why the New Testament was only inaugurated on the day of Pentecost, under the direct shadow of the cross.

### Hearing: the Key to a life of faith in the power of the Spirit.

> *"This only I want to learn from you: Did you receive the Spirit by the works of the law or by the hearing of faith?"* (3:2)

> *"Therefore He who supplies the Spirit to you and works miracles among you, does He do it by the works of the law or by the hearing of faith?"* (3:5)

These verses indicate the source of faith: the hearing faculty. Romans underlines this: "Faith comes by hearing." (Rom. 10:17). This is one of the most overlooked verses in this precious book, namely that faith is not a product of human striving. Faith simply comes. (See also Galatians 3:23 "faith came" and 3:25 "faith has come.") Faith is not the fruit of the exercise of our will, nor the power of intellect, though these faculties have their role to play. In order for faith to be born in a heart, we must simply quieten our hearts and minds and listen to the voice of the Spirit. This is the hardest discipline of all, and yet the most necessary. The hearts of men and women are spiritually bankrupt, and nothing good can come from within. The great need is to hear God's voice. This can seem very exclusive, as it is very rare for someone to hear an audible voice. But the hearing of faith is not hearing an audible voice; it is rather an inner consciousness that is imparted initially when we hear the gospel.

For those who are saved it is an inner persuasion that dawns in our hearts as we wait on God. We wait and without knowing how or exactly when, we are persuaded of something, we know something. Faith is given to the listening heart, and it is to the listening heart that the Holy Spirit is given. It is through such a heart that miracles are done. Jesus Himself demonstrates this truth in absolute perfection. One can describe His whole inner life as calm quiet listening to the whisper of the Father. That Christ had a soul at peace and rest is simply foundational. No one can be close to God with inner noise and turmoil. Christ asserted that He did nothing unless prompted and led by His Father (John 5:19-20). This is to be as true in our lives, as it was in His.

This whole section of Galatians goes to the heart of spiritual life. We either live from our own inner resources, or we listen to God, we lean on Him, we draw from His presence in our hearts. The Christian life will typically go through three phases: first the knowledge that "CHRIST IS FOR ME." Secondly there is a stirring to respond, and we come to "I FOR CHRIST." This then leads to the third greatest discovery of all: "CHRIST IN ME."

Just as Paul has described the two great blessings of Abraham as Justification and the baptism with the Holy Spirit, he also describes in this section the great curse of the Law.

> *"For as many as are of the works of the law are under the curse; for it is written, "Cursed is everyone who does not continue in all things which are written in the book of the law to do them.""* (3:10)

Paul is showing us that if we live as Christians from our own resources, then we shall feel constant condemnation. The law produces a sense of failure. So, why did God give the Law?

## The Law is our tutor to bring us to God

Paul again restates that the promise of the Messiah predates the law, when God vowed that Abraham's seed should inherit the promise (Gal 3:16). The Law then was a temporary interlude to teach Israel and the human race the utter powerlessness of men and women to gain acceptance with God through self effort. The law produced a sense of our sin and by this brought us to Christ.

The law did not provide a means to reconcile a Holy God and sinful humanity. The Law is built on mediation by a third party. This is against God's perfect plan, for God is one, and cannot accept any mediating power between Him and man (Gal 3:20). Christ is the perfect mediator, because He is also Himself God, and is reconciling the world to Himself: "God was in Christ reconciling the world to Himself." (2 Cor. 5:19).

The Law then convicts of sin so that sinners may turn to God and cast themselves in faith on His mercy (Gal 3:22). The Law then was not simply the tutor of Israel historically keeping

Israel under condemnation for fifteen hundred years from Moses till Christ! The Law was the personal tutor of every individual Israelite, to make them aware of their sin, and lead them to come in faith to the living God. All true believers who were under the Law of Moses, from Moses himself right through to John Baptist, were convicted of sin by the law's demands, and brought to repentance, humility and faith.

# CHAPTER 4

## *From slavery to Sonship*
## *Galatians 4:1-7*

> *[1] Now I say that the heir, as long as he is a child, does not differ at all from a slave, though he is master of all, [2] but is under guardians and stewards until the time appointed by the father. [3] Even so we, when we were children, were in bondage under the elements of the world. [4] But when the fullness of the time had come, God sent forth His Son, born of a woman, born under the law, [5] to redeem those who were under the law, that we might receive the adoption as sons.*
>
> *[6] And because you are sons, God has sent forth the Spirit of His Son into your hearts, crying out, "Abba, Father!" [7] Therefore you are no longer a slave but a son, and if a son, then an heir of God through Christ.*

Chapter 4 begins with an illustration from the culture and time in which Paul lived. He refers to the custom where a son was brought up in much the manner of a slave, until the day in which he passed from childhood to adulthood. On that day the son would be taken by the father into a public place and there publicly declared to be his son. Before this day, the son was under tutors and governors, who made sure that the son made good progress in all areas of learning.

Paul uses this illustration to explain that humanity was in its spiritual infancy until the coming of Christ. Up until His coming, we were living in shadows of spiritual life and not in the reality. Access to spiritual reality was limited in the Old Testament, awaiting the power and effect of the cross to change human nature through regeneration. The Law was God's mercy to sinners, to help each individual find God in the fog of an unregenerate nature. Until we could be renewed by the Spirit unto real spiritual life, we had to be helped by outward forms, including animal sacrifices, the use of special buildings such as the tabernacle and the temple. All these things were full of spiritual meaning, and yet taken together they indicated that the way into a deeper relationship with God was still not open:

> *"The Holy Spirit indicating this, that the way into the Holiest of All was not yet made manifest while the first tabernacle was still standing. It was symbolic ... concerned only with foods and drinks, various washings, and fleshly ordinances imposed until the time of reformation."* (Heb. 9:8-10).

Just as mankind was in its spiritual infancy, so too can individuals remain in infancy until reaching the spiritual reality of finding Christ. A person can unwittingly live in religious shadows – a state which cannot satisfy the heart's true longing. This state is declared by Paul to be a state of bondage, from which there is a deep longing to be set free. This bondage can be seen in some traditional churches where the liberating power of the Spirit has not been known. Gloom and sadness can colour religion which lacks spiritual reality.

What then is this spiritual reality? The answer is given in this chapter in two distinct phases: first the coming of Jesus; second the coming of the Spirit.

> *"But when the fullness of the time had come, God sent forth his Son, born of a woman, born under the law" (4:4)*

With these words, Paul introduces the end of bondage - *"God sent forth His Son."* In Christ there were no shadows or forms of truth. He was the perfect image of the Father's person, the brightness of His glory shining out in clarity. Jesus is not a stage of revelation. He was God living on earth in flesh and blood. He declared life without bondage. Whatever bondages there may be in human beings, Christ revealed the wonder of a free life; free from law, free from sin, free from religion, guilt, shame and demons. Christ is the declaration of God's will for humanity; that we might live like Him. The revelation of Jesus created intense longing in His followers to be like Him. His disciples left everything to be with Him. At the same time, He exposed the shallowness of religion in form without power or substance.

The Pharisees had embraced the Old Testament and out of it had created a robe of pride and superiority for themselves. Christ exposed them as babies playing with toys, fooling themselves and others, as if through their robes, their grand buildings and their titles, they had some great standing before God. It is often forgotten that the civil authority did not arrest and try Jesus; it was the chief priests that plotted His arrest, and condemned Him to death. They used the civil authorities to carry out the death sentence. The sin of Pilate was that he allowed Himself to be used for the greatest injustice ever perpetrated by the human race. But Pilate's sin lay in his moral cowardice and indifference. He felt no envy towards Jesus, and would have preferred to set him free. The greatest enemy of the truth of God is not in the world, but in religious men who have not discovered the realm of spiritual reality in Christ.

## *Fears for the Church*
## *Galatians 4:8-20*

*⁸ But then, indeed, when you did not know God, you served those which by nature are not gods. ⁹ But now after you have known God, or rather are known by God, how is it that you turn again to the weak and beggarly elements, to which you desire again to be in bondage? ¹⁰ You observe days and months and seasons and years. ¹¹ I am afraid for you, lest I have laboured for you in vain.*

*¹² Brethren, I urge you to become like me, for I became like you. You have not injured me at all. ¹³ You know that because of physical infirmity I preached the gospel to you at the first. ¹⁴ And my trial which was in my flesh you did not despise or reject, but you received me as an angel of God, even as Christ Jesus. ¹⁵ What then was the blessing you enjoyed? For I bear you witness that, if possible, you would have plucked out your own eyes and given them to me. ¹⁶ Have I therefore become your enemy because I tell you the truth?*

*¹⁷ They zealously court you, but for no good; yes, they want to exclude you, that you may be zealous for them. ¹⁸ But it is good to be zealous in a good thing always, and not only when I am present with you. ¹⁹ My little children, for whom I labour in birth again until Christ is formed in you, ²⁰ I would like to be present with you now and to change my tone; for I have doubts about you.*

The second stage of spiritual reality is the coming of the Spirit to make us children of God. In verses 5 and 6, Paul says that we receive adoption as sons when the Spirit floods our hearts, causing us to cry from deep within "Abba - Father!" He explains this further by the phrase "Now, after that you have known God or rather are known by God." (4:9). Spiritual reality is fellowship with God Himself, not with pictures and symbols that portray God. The Spirit comes and fills a heart, setting us as children in His kingdom, filling us with the intimate awareness of God Himself. Religious practice becomes irrelevant to the heart flooding with the unspeakable joy of the presence of God. Knowing God is the foundation of eternal life:

> *"This is eternal life that they may know You, the only true God, and Jesus Christ whom You have sent,"* John 17:3.

Once again, a tiny phrase hidden in this letter contains a vast spiritual principle. The key to life is to know God and to be known by God. This is the basis of judgment itself, since the most condemning words from the lips of Jesus are "I never knew you." (Matt 7:23; Matt 25:12; 2 Tim 2:19). The emphasis is on God knowing us, and at first sight this seems odd, since doesn't God know everything? But the truth is that eternal life is based on a restoration of fellowship between God and humanity, by which we become friends of God through Jesus. It is possible to live with someone for fifty years and not know them. The only way to know and be known is to bare the heart, to tell it all, and let God into the deep intimate secrets of our hearts. It is vital that this key to salvation be understood. It is not the pursuit of power, it is the pursuit of a loving relationship, and can be summed up in a single phrase: make friends with Jesus! This alone explains how someone may perform miracles, speak with tongues or cast out demons and yet still be strangers to Jesus (Matt 7:21-23).

The sadness of this chapter is that Paul is keenly aware that the Galatian Christians had abandoned this liberating relationship with Christ to return to the shadowy religious practices of the law. He speaks of blessings that they used to have. He reminds them of the circumstances of his first visit, when he lingered long with them because he had been sick among them (Galatians 4:13-15). He reminds them that they had become so appreciative of his ministry that they would have plucked out their own eyes if they could have replaced Paul's sick eyes. They had been filled with overwhelming love for God's servant.

How tragic it is that so many are capable of looking back on times when God blessed them, and yet now are living again in the shadows. Paul is longing for these believers, in an agony of heart and prayer, until Christ be formed in them again (verse 19). Notice here that Christ had been formed in their hearts when they first believed. But they had not gone on in this new life. Now they needed the first foundations to be renewed in them. What a promise lies in this prayer! When the Spirit comes, bringing the reality of the knowledge of Christ, at that very moment, a resemblance to Christ Himself is formed in the believer's heart. Truly the baptism with the Spirit is deeper and fuller than many of us have ever suspected.

## Which Covenant do we live under: Old or New?
## Galatians 4:21-31

> *21 Tell me, you who desire to be under the law, do you not hear the law? 22 For it is written that Abraham had two sons: the one by a bondwoman, the other by a freewoman. 23 But he who was of the bondwoman was born according to the flesh, and he of the freewoman through promise, 24 which things are symbolic. For these are the two covenants: the one from Mount Sinai which gives birth to bondage, which is Hagar— 25 for this Hagar is Mount Sinai in Arabia, and corresponds to Jerusalem which now is, and is in bondage with her children— 26 but the Jerusalem above is free, which is the mother of us all. 27 For it is written:*
>
> *"Rejoice, O barren, you who do not bear! Break forth and shout, you who are not in labour! For the desolate has many more children than she who has a husband."*
>
> *28 Now we, brethren, as Isaac was, are children of promise. 29 But, as he who was born according to the flesh then persecuted him who was born according to the Spirit, even so it is now. 30 Nevertheless what does the Scripture say? "Cast out the bondwoman and her son, for the son of the bondwoman shall not be heir with the son of the freewoman." 31 So then, brethren, we are not children of the bondwoman but of the free.*

Paul explains the matter further by reference to the two sons of Abraham, which are pictures of these two states of heart and of the two covenants. Ishmael is a picture of man in bondage to outward religious practices, while Isaac is the son of the promise, the one in whom God's promises are fulfilled. Hagar and Ishmael correspond to earthly Jerusalem, which is in bondage with her children. Ishmael was born into the home of Abraham through Abraham's fear that God was not able to fulfil His promise supernaturally. He doubted the power of God, and decided to help God fulfil His great plan. When Ishmael was finally born, there was no joy in the home, since both Abraham and Sarah knew deep down that there was nothing miraculous about this birth. It was the product of their own scheming, and their own strength. Ishmael brought sadness and division, and though God extended mercy to the boy, and blessed him, yet he could never be a symbol of God's true grace, and had to be cast out.

But Isaac was a pure miracle. He was a true demonstration of what God can do in the believing heart. God seeks those who will dare to believe Him and take Him at His word, as impossible as it may seem at first. Like Abraham, each one must recognise the feebleness of our own efforts, and acknowledge the need of God's power in our lives through the Holy Spirit. We are to step out of playing at Christianity into the realm of likeness to Christ, and of a real vibrant relationship with God.

What are the things that prevent us from experiencing this blessing? The greatest enemy is pride. The Bible promises that the Christian life is one of rest without any trophies to crown our human ability. The gospel offers no room for us to boast. It is the inner battle with our ego that holds back spiritual fulfilment. It is only slowly that we understand that pride is the greatest enemy.

And then there is the most exhausting enemy of all: a divided heart. The attraction of the world, disobedience, bitterness, hurts etc... all these things entering in can choke the word and we become unfruitful, like the seed sown among thorns in Jesus' parable. Some have just enough Christianity to spoil their enjoyment of the world, but not enough to find the joy of rich friendship with Christ.

The most subtle enemy is unbelief. There must be conviction and inner persuasion of what God has said in order to claim the life He offers as our own. This is why the writer to the Hebrews exhorts his readers to come boldly to the throne of grace, and to enter the holiest place of all with confidence. God has promised spiritual reality in His Son and through the power of the Holy Spirit. Let us then boldly enter in.

## The Glory of the Everlasting Covenant.

Many of these verses are so disarmingly familiar to readers of the New Testament that their impact may be lost. In Hebrews 13:20-21 we read:

> *"Now may the God of peace who brought up our Lord Jesus from the dead, that great Shepherd of the sheep, through the blood of the everlasting covenant, make you complete in every good work to do His will, working in you what is well pleasing in His sight, through Jesus Christ, to whom be glory for ever and ever. Amen."*

The phrase that stands out is *"the everlasting covenant."* This is a further description of the "New Covenant" and introduces us to the fact that though the new covenant is experienced as a means of salvation from sin, yet it has an eternal context that far transcends time. The everlasting covenant is through the blood of Jesus, by which we understand that this covenant is as everlasting as God Himself and is part of His nature and being.

What was the nature of the everlasting covenant before man was introduced to it? There was obviously no written agreement between the three persons of the Godhead. The covenant that binds them together is a bond of perpetual love written in their their life blood. The three persons of the Godhead are constantly poured out for one another in living sacrifice, honouring and serving one another in flawless never-ending love. There is no cross in God, no nails, no thorns, but there is the love that will pour itself out to the point of death when need arises. The marvel of the new covenant is that human beings become partakers of the same life and nature that is in God. Humanity is grafted into the Godhead by the blood of the covenant. Humanity does not become divine, but is indwelt by the divine life of God Himself. The act of God in opening the veins of His son was an act of stupendous daring, to open a door for sinners to approach and enter into the very heart of God.

*"I have been crucified with Christ..."* (Galatians 2:20)

These words are perhaps the most sublime ever written and they express what lies at the centre of the New Covenant. They describe the incredible fact that, by the grace of God, we are ushered into the place where God's love reached its greatest expression. Salvation is eternally secure because we are made to partake of the foundations of God's life. The amazing fact about God is that He *is* love, and such a love that empties itself, and pours itself out for others. The child of God has been rooted in the same quality of life that makes God so amazing. In other words, His incredible life is in us. It is not only that we have God's love in our hearts; but we have the purest love - the love of Calvary - poured into us.

This is what makes the child of God so much more than Adam was even in Eden. Adam had the potential to have fellowship with God, and thus to let God fill him with this love. But the sinner can **only** be saved by the love of Calvary. This love is the door, and then we discover that it is the essence of God's Being, and that we are called to fellowship with God continually in this love, and to manifest it. God does not ask us to attain the love of Calvary; He has given us that love as a gift. All we must do is believe and let that love flow.

# CHAPTER 5

## *The choice: a life of love or a life of sin*
## *Galatians 5:1-15*

> [1] Stand fast therefore in the liberty by which Christ has made us free, and do not be entangled again with a yoke of bondage. [2] Indeed I, Paul, say to you that if you become circumcised, Christ will profit you nothing. [3] And I testify again to every man who becomes circumcised that he is a debtor to keep the whole law. [4] You have become estranged from Christ, you who attempt to be justified by law; you have fallen from grace. [5] For we through the Spirit eagerly wait for the hope of righteousness by faith. [6] For in Christ Jesus neither circumcision nor uncircumcision avails anything, but faith working through love.
>
> [7] You ran well. Who hindered you from obeying the truth? [8] This persuasion does not come from Him who calls you. [9] A little leaven leavens the whole lump. [10] I have confidence in you, in the Lord, that you will have no other mind; but he who troubles you shall bear his judgment, whoever he is.
>
> [11] And I, brethren, if I still preach circumcision, why do I still suffer persecution? Then the offense of the cross has

> *ceased. ¹² I could wish that those who trouble you would even cut themselves off!*
>
> *¹³ For you, brethren, have been called to liberty; only do not use liberty as an opportunity for the flesh, but through love serve one another. ¹⁴ For all the law is fulfilled in one word, even in this: "You shall love your neighbour as yourself." ¹⁵ But if you bite and devour one another, beware lest you be consumed by one another!*

It is in this chapter that Paul places before the Christian the stark choice between the flesh and the Spirit. Many Christians like to think of themselves as living on the frontier between these two realms. They are in the Spirit from time to time and sometimes make choices in the flesh, which they acknowledge sheepishly as not being quite the best. But Paul is here declaring that as soon as we allow this mixture we become burdened again with the yoke of slavery. A foundational principle of all New Testament thought is repeated in this chapter:

> *"A little leaven leavens the whole lump" (5:9)*

In 1 Cor. 5:6 the leaven refers to sin. Here in Galatians it is referring to doctrine. Mix a little legalism into the life in the Spirit and you have complete corruption.

Paul is quite categorical:

> *"Indeed I, Paul, say to you that if you become circumcised, Christ will profit you nothing." (5:2)*

Such a state is a fallen one, that is; we have fallen away from grace. (5:4). In this condition we are unable to benefit from the person of Christ and the power of His redemption. And the cause of this disaster? - quite simply: circumcision. This ritual signalled a shift in their doctrinal position; the way they thought about God and his power to save them. Circumcision indicated that they no longer believed Christ to be all they needed to save them. The Galatian Christians needed a radical return to the foundations of Christian living. This chapter itself turns on the conflict between life in the flesh and life in the Spirit. Both realms are exposed thus enabling the reader to discern where his life is rooted.

## *Life in the flesh.*
## *Galatians 5:16-26*

> *16 I say then: Walk in the Spirit, and you shall not fulfil the lust of the flesh. 17 For the flesh lusts against the Spirit, and the Spirit against the flesh; and these are contrary to one another, so that you do not do the things that you wish. 18 But if you are led by the Spirit, you are not under the law.*
>
> *19 Now the works of the flesh are evident, which are: adultery, fornication, uncleanness, lewdness, 20 idolatry, sorcery, hatred, contentions, jealousies, outbursts of wrath, selfish ambitions, dissensions, heresies, 21 envy, murders, drunkenness, revelries, and the like; of which I tell you beforehand, just as I also told you in time past, that those who practice such things will not inherit the kingdom of God.*

When Paul speaks of *"the flesh"*, he does not mean merely the physical realm. The word flesh is used in the New Testament in two distinct senses that can be clearly seen by quoting two scriptures:

> *"And the Word was made flesh, and dwelt among us, (and we beheld His glory, the glory as of the only begotten of the Father,) full of grace and truth" (John 1:14)*
>
> *"But you are not in the flesh, but in the Spirit, if indeed the Spirit of God dwells in you." (Romans 8:9)*

John says that the everlasting Word became flesh, referring to the miracle of the incarnation. But Paul says of the Christians in Rome that they were not in the flesh! This cannot mean that they had ceased to be flesh and blood, but refers to the fact that they were no longer living under the power of a sinful, carnal nature. Paul in Galatians chapter 5 is once more speaking of sinful human nature, from which a person is freed when the Holy Spirit lives in them.

When a Christian lives in *"the flesh"*, he or she is cut off from the power of redemption, from the wonder of the life of Christ; and all the power of sin stirs in their heart again. The full power of the flesh is revealed in the awful list of sins listed in these verses. *(5:19-21)*

Paul is laying before the believer the awful symptoms of legalism. The first one is in the sexual domain, and does not necessarily mean the practice of sexual sin, but rather that the individual is obsessed with it, never free from it. But then he goes on to explain how legalism spawns jealousies and rivalries among Christians, leading to bitter, murderous thoughts, and rebellious attitudes. He also traces major doctrinal heresies back to the flesh, leading to the obvious conclusion that one can expect doctrinal imbalance to go hand in hand with lustful imaginations which can lead to flagrant or secret sin. Finally Paul includes "revelries," i.e. superficiality, self-indulgence and pleasure-seeking, as manifestations of the flesh. Are these perhaps the most dangerous sins for some

Christians as they are not so obviously bad, and present no glaring evidence of wrong living?

Furthermore in the centre of this chapter, Paul expects that carnal living will have a devastating effect on church life:

> *"But if you bite and devour one another, beware lest you be consumed by one another!" (5:15)*

There will be arguments, destructive exchanges with cruel, spiteful and hurtful words. These lead to divisions, splits and the destruction of once living churches. Many deep problems in churches can be traced back to this source, that men and women are living in the flesh. It can then be concluded that if only we would be broken and humbled in deep repentance, divisions would be healed and the life-giving presence of God restored. Let us walk with God in love and humility in times of hurt and division in a church. There is a way for each one to walk with God even through the worst circumstances.

The Galatians were in danger of living in the flesh through two opposite temptations:

**1. Law - Circumcision.** This was doctrinal, leading the church to believe in a physical sign that made them accepted as God's people. All such belief is misplaced. No outward pattern of behaviour can save us. Salvation is only by total and complete trust in Christ alone. It is for this reason that many experience a mixed kind of life, because they will not forsake their belief that they can and must contribute something to their salvation (Ephesians 2:8-9). This undermines the work of the Spirit, who ministers joy and peace as gifts of grace, not as rewards for good effort. The only "reward" for effort is carnal smug self-satisfaction that blinds the heart to true grace.

This is a very subtle danger and yet all the more deadly for that. Baptism, church going, communion, bible reading and prayer - all of these are important and biblical practices. Yet to trust in any of them as the grounds of my acceptance before God dislodges my soul from the place of grace. Everyone must maintain a walk with God whereby we are reliant on the grace of God and the power of the Holy Spirit. The most experienced intercessor needs as much aid in prayer as the beginner. God's people are granted grace to live - they live by the faith that God supplies.

**2. License - False liberty.** In declaring that righteousness does not come through the law, Paul warns the Galatians that this does not liberate them to self-indulgent living:

> *"For you, brethren, have been called to liberty; only do not [use] liberty as an opportunity for the flesh, but through love serve one another." (5:13)*

Liberty from the law does not mean anything goes, rather it means that all is permissible that is rooted in relationship with Christ through the Spirit. The same is equally true of food, drink, and clothing. *"Eat drink and be merry"* is indicative of a shallow kind of living in which pleasure is found in these realms. Many turn to food rather than to God. Many have delicacies at hand to distract them from the profound emptiness of their living. But shallow carnal habits lead to eruptions of anger and inner tensions that stir in the heart of the person who is not centred on Christ. It is time once more that Christians made up their minds whom they will serve: Myself, or the great King of Heaven? Liberty is the freedom at last to do what is right, not to do what I want.

## *Life in the Spirit.*
## *Galatians 5:22-26*

> 22 But the fruit of the Spirit is love, joy, peace, longsuffering, kindness, goodness, faithfulness, 23 gentleness, self-control. Against such there is no law. 24 And those who are Christ's have crucified the flesh with its passions and desires. 25 If we live in the Spirit, let us also walk in the Spirit. 26 Let us not become conceited, provoking one another, envying one another.

This chapter gives three keys to life in the Spirit, which are of vital importance to our whole understanding of the Christian life. The great danger is to transfer principles of natural living into the realm of spiritual living. For example, each person must **earn** their daily bread; they must have employment which has its financial rewards. An individual will then build up his resources, buying a house, etc... But in the realm of the Spirit there is to be no work in order to advance spiritually. Rather each individual must ensure that their life is in the right attitude for the grace of God to produce growth. What then are these three keys to spiritual living?

## 1. The life in the Spirit is a life of love.

> *"For all the law is fulfilled in one word, even in this: "You shall love your neighbour as yourself." (5:14)*

This is a definition of a truly spiritual man or woman: one who truly loves. Love is not an attribute of God. God is love. He can never be anything else. Therefore all of God's attributes are attributes of love. Similarly, love is not to be an attribute of the Christian or a work, love is to be the ceaseless spring from which all of life flows. Without love a person is not a Christian, without love a church is not a church. A Christian without love is a monster, a lamb with the heart of a wolf, at best an image in stone, with a vague suggestion of something beautiful but no direct experience of it. Love is without hurt or harm, it produces an inner calm in which other lives are welcome and held in warmth and tenderness. Love scatters fears, reassures doubters, and spreads joy in all it meets. There are kind words to answer harsh ones, there are loving thoughts to refresh the soul. Love is not a work, though countless works flow from it. It colours every action, every deed, and makes everything a manifestation of that most perfect life - Jesus the Son of God.

Some wander from this path and think of life in the Spirit as a life of power. The centre of things can easily become what we achieve for God, we become performance orientated, measuring our value to God and others by the statistics - how many meetings held, how many souls won, how much fasting and prayer. All of these things are wonderful but they are not life in the Spirit. The greatest power in the realm of the Spirit is the power of love. Men and women give up, even the most determined, and the most heroic, but love goes on for ever. Love carries within itself the power of self renewal, for it never runs out. The greater the flow, the greater the resources seem to be. Love is attractive, seeping into the chinks of the stoutest armour. Love wins hardened cynics, and conquers stubborn rebels. It is in this realm that Christians are to live, and it is the cry of all who really look for the kingdom of God.

Lord! Make me love as God Himself is love!

## 2. The life is a fruit.

The great question then is "How can I love?" The answer to this lies in one of the Bible's greatest statements:

> *"But the fruit of the Spirit is love, joy, peace, longsuffering, kindness, goodness, faithfulness, gentleness, self-control. Against such there is no law."* (5:22-23)

Love is the fruit of the Spirit. The Christian life cannot be likened to a factory producing identical cans of baked beans or cars. People use methods to produce their goods; they need machinery, investment, and power etc... Some churches and movements seem to operate on this kind of principle! But the truth is that all our efforts cannot alter the motivation of the human heart, nor produce a single atom of love. If there is no love in the heart, then all my striving and tears and pleading will not change my state.

Love is a fruit, and therefore two things are required to produce it: seed ... and the right conditions for growth. If I am to grow in the life of the Spirit, then I must receive living seed from God, and keep my heart in the right conditions for that seed to flourish and grow. This is quite consistent with the teaching of Jesus in the parable of the sower and other parables where the power of growth lies in the seed itself, while the receiver does not understand how the seed grows (Mark 4:26-28). He cannot hurry it; he can only patiently nourish and cherish it.

The Christian life then is to be likened to a plant that grows. It cannot be transplanted as a ready grown plant. Growth cannot be imitated, by intensive Bible courses or Bible schools. These things have their place, but they cannot substitute spiritual growth. So what is the seed? The answer lies here in Galatians:

> *"Now to Abraham and his Seed were the promises made. He does not say, "And to seeds," as of many; but as of one, "And to your Seed, which is Christ." (3:16)*

Christ Himself is the Seed. It is not enough for us to make a decision to follow Christ or to seek to follow His teaching; we must receive Christ deep into our beings, as our life. The apostle Paul says:

> "For me to live is Christ" (Philippians 1:21),
>
> "Christ, [who is] our life" (Colossians 3:4)

It is this union with Christ that is the foundation of our new life. Christ cannot create love in a human heart, for that would not be love. It would be a beautiful decoration, but not an integrated part of the life. Human beings alone cannot produce love, as their efforts have mixed motives. Our love runs out and fades with sustained opposition, revealing that there are stronger powers in our hearts such as self and pride. We must recognise how love is formed in us or we may wander fruitless through a wilderness all our lives.

It is impossible to manufacture love, but the love of God pours into our hearts as we meet Jesus Christ.

> "In this is love, not that we loved God, but that He loved us and sent His son to be the propitiation for our sins." (1 John 4:10)

As we yield to the love of God in Christ and surrender to Him, he floods us with the Spirit:

> "...the love of God has been poured out in our hearts by the Holy Spirit who was given unto us." (Romans 5:5)

Then, as we bathe in His love in wonder, gratitude and delight, we become aware that something new is appearing in our hearts, like a tender shoot from a dry root. It is exquisite – it is our love for Him.

### *3. The presence of God is the atmosphere of growth.*

So far Paul has identified that love must be our life, and that this life is a plant that grows from the seed which is Christ Himself. The perfect conditions for this life to grow are God's own life-giving Presence. When Paul uses the phrase "in the Spirit" it must be understood that he is referring to conscious abiding in the Presence of God. The whole purpose of the baptism with the Holy Spirit is that it is the introduction of a person into the realm of living in God's presence.

The great enemy of God's presence is my own presence. Imagine a person being allowed to be seated at a banquet next to the President of the United States. They would have the unique opportunity to have an exchange of views. They would have to think through the opportunity. Some might use it to apply for the correction of some injustice. Others might use it as a chance to put over their own views on some hot political topic. Without any doubt, the greatest use of the time would be to make the President so enjoy the experience, that he invited you back! The worst result would be to embarrass everyone so that you were asked to leave or be quiet!

In the same way, when we come into the presence of God, the most important thing is to hush my own thoughts and feelings and lift up the Lord Himself. The way into the deep things of God is through death to self. God's presence is itself deadly to lustful, selfish attitudes. None of us can get far in this kingdom unless we are willing to lose everything in order to progress. The further I go, the lighter my burdens become. The further I go, the less I carry. Paul describes the pursuit of God's presence as being the activity of "forgetting" and "reaching forward." (Philippians 3:13)

If these three principles are understood and embraced, Christians will experience the wonder of Christ being formed in their lives and then outworked and revealed in their conduct.

Christ Himself summed up this teaching in one brief phrase: "Abide in Me." (John 15:4).

## Walking in the Spirit – overcoming the flesh.

These three principles are the basis of walking with God. In this passage Paul gives an astonishingly simple formula for overcoming our sinful nature (the flesh):

*"Walk in the Spirit and you shall not fulfil the lusts of the flesh," (Galatians 5:16)*

*"Walk in love, as Christ also has loved us," (Ephesians 5:2)*

Amazingly it is not by confronting our base desires that we overcome them. Yes we must forsake and turn our backs on them. But the power to overcome is in the positive action of looking at Jesus and obeying the whisper of the Spirit in our conscience. We walk in the Spirit as we guard and wait on God's presence in us and treasure the life giving perfume of His love.

As we do these things, sin loses its stranglehold over us, and the tormenting control of carnal desires evaporates in the face of the pure desires that arise in the atmosphere of the Holy Spirit. If we confront our sinful tendencies without the Presence of God we find ourselves quickly entangled in a conflict we cannot win. We might well be able to control our behaviour outwardly, but inside we are unable to overcome the thoughts and feelings that defile us. The Lord does not give us a series of options on how to overcome the flesh, He gives us only one: walking in the Spirit. Overcoming is not through our strength of resolve, but rather through an obedient will. We must not "whine" about the power of the flesh, but turn our backs on it and walk by faith in sensitivity to the presence of the Lord through the Holy Spirit.

Walking is by its very nature a matter of patience and steady persistence. Paul said that carnality was a sign of spiritual immaturity:

*"I could not speak to you as to spiritual people but as to carnal, as to babes in Christ,"* (1 Corinthians 3:1)

This is comforting to know that we are not expected to learn to walk overnight. Babies struggle to stand in the first year of life and then take their first step. As they persevere, they do it at last without thinking. So it is with the things of the Spirit. At first we must apply ourselves diligently to guard our hearts and work out His inner presence through loving actions. As we do this, walking in the Spirit and walking in love will become our habit of life and we will be solid, mature Christians.

*"...those who are Christ's have crucified the flesh with its passions and desires."* (Galatians 5:24)

We do not need to have a hammer and nails in our hands to fulfil this verse, but we do need to have fervency of spirit, and to absolutely forsake a self-centred and pleasure-centred life, in order to attain the goal of a Christ-centred life.

There was no mercy in the act of crucifixion, and the Christian must not deal mercifully with sin, in whatever form it may present itself to us. If we deal with temptation casually, we shall find no mercy in the flesh - it will bite the hand that feeds it. Victory is never far from us - it is only a turn away. We must turn our back on sin, forsaking it with all our heart, and receiving that fragrant perfume of Christ.

Once His Presence touches us, we are instantly aware that the flesh is totally powerless before Him. If we try and face two directions, the flesh will instantly triumph. The power to walk in the Spirit is given to us, so all we must do is turn to Him with all our hearts and walk.

When we walk in the Spirit we may not at first realise that we have instantly overcome the flesh, because God's way is to fill our vision with Himself causing us to overcome by keeping our eyes on Him, not on our temptations.

# CHAPTER 6

## *Bearing and sharing the burdens*
## *Galatians 6:1-5*

> *¹ Brethren, if a man is overtaken in any trespass, you who are spiritual restore such a one in a spirit of gentleness, considering yourself lest you also be tempted. ² Bear one another's burdens, and so fulfil the law of Christ. ³ For if anyone thinks himself to be something, when he is nothing, he deceives himself. ⁴ But let each one examine his own work, and then he will have rejoicing in himself alone, and not in another. ⁵ For each one shall bear his own load.*

Free indeed at last, and truly free. Not only that, but through grace alone. But grace must produce graciousness, or it is only another ideal: lovely, admirable, but quite powerless. Grace must produce real kindness in practical life. The way we live reveals what we really believe, and how deeply our beliefs have mastered our hearts and become our life.

Paul's starting point in this section is the way we deal with a brother or sister who fails to meet standards of morality. Nothing can be more real than the way we think, speak and feel about "fallen sinners." It is the great test of our consciousness and understanding of grace. There is much to test us in this realm: whether it be the failings of new converts, or the more serious matter of sin in the lives of pastors and ministers. It also includes our attitude to politicians and other public figures. There is no doubt how society reacts to scandal: with fascination and delight. Of course the world loves to see Christians lose their temper, tell white lies, and indulge in worldly pursuits. All these things confirm them in their view that Christians are not genuine. But most of all, worldly people enjoy the embarrassment of a minister of the gospel found guilty of adultery.

> *Jim Bakker was a famous American TV evangelist, but who fell into immorality, and fraud. He was convicted and sentenced to 45 years in prison.*
>
> *While there, he was asked in an interview: "Who was the biggest surprise visitor you had in prison?"*
>
> *Answer: "Billy Graham was the biggest surprise because he is such a busy man. A few days before he arrived he had been voted the most respected man in the world. I heard that on my little radio in prison. He came just a few days before I found out that my wife was divorcing me. So I think it was God preparing me for that moment. When he came to visit me I had the flu. I looked like a man who had slept under a bridge. My hair was a mess and I had my old toilet-cleaning clothes on. My toes were sticking out of my shoes. I had just finished cleaning the toilets, and the guards came to get me. One of the guards led me across the compound, and I thought he was taking me to the lieutenant's office. I thought maybe I was in trouble. But then they said, "Didn't they tell you. Billy Graham is here to see you."*

*So I walked into the room and he had his arms outstretched and he embraced me and told me he loved me. We sat and talked, and when he prayed everyone else in the room prayed. When you feel like you're worthless, and then somebody like that comes, it's really shocking.*

*As soon as I was released from prison, Ruth Graham called the Salvation Army halfway house where I was and asked permission for me to go to church with her that Sunday morning. When I got there, the pastor welcomed me and sat me with the Graham clan—two whole rows of them. I'd only been out of prison 48 hours. The organ began playing and Ruth walked down the aisle and sat next to inmate 07407-058, telling the world that I was her friend.*

*Afterwards, she had me up to their cabin for dinner. When she asked me for some addresses, I pulled this envelope out of my pocket to look for them. In prison you're not allowed to have a wallet, so you just carry an envelope. She asked, "Don't you have a wallet?" And I said, "Well, yeah, this is my wallet." After five years of brainwashing in prison you think an envelope is a wallet. She walked into the other room, came back, and said, "Here's one of Billy's wallets. He doesn't need it. You can have it."*

*The Grahams sponsored me, paid for a house for me to live in, and gave me a car to drive.*

*Adapted from: Christianity Today (12/7/98)*

When heads of government sin and fail as in the case of President Clinton's relationship with Monica Lewinsky, the dogs are unleashed and the worst details are repeated endlessly. Hearts that react in these ways know nothing of grace. The world condemns, while the heart that knows grace grieves and prays. The selfish heart reacts with smug satisfaction and a sense of superiority, but when our hearts are touched by grace, we have glimpsed into the abyss of our own sinful powers, and yet have received the unmerited kindness of God to liberate us through forgiveness and cleansing. Then we cannot condemn others. A judgmental heart and repentance are opposites. They cannot exist together.

> *"Brethren, if a man is overtaken in any trespass, you who are spiritual, restore such a one in a spirit of gentleness, considering yourself, lest you also be tempted. Bear one another's burdens and so fulfil the law of Christ." (6:1-2)*

There is great humility in this attitude, as the apostle expresses the awareness that any one of us can sin, if we are exposed to temptation. Our objective as those who walk in the Spirit should be to bring sinful people back into fellowship with God. Therefore our approach to them is in meekness and loving kindness. We must beware of hardening our attitude into moral arrogance. We can become so unchrist-like that we are of no use to help any sinner. Paul says that it is in this attitude of love that we fulfil the requirements of Christ for His people. This is the fulfilment of the law: love. When a man is in need, and we go to his aid, it is then that we please Christ. Jim Bakker, the founder of the PTL ministry in America, committed serious fraud, collecting money from Christians and misusing it. He was sentenced to 45 years in prison, and began his prison term as a broken man. The press and many Christians condemned him, but Billy Graham visited him in prison several times. There can be no doubt who helped him to find hope in Christ again. Billy Graham saw in Jim Bakker a man staggering under the burden of moral failure and ran to help him.

It is of importance to note at the end of verse two that it is this very act of sharing burdens which is the fulfilment of the "law of Christ." Paul uses here a phrase that would for some have contrasted with the "Law of Moses". Christ's law is that of positive love, rather than a list of "do nots." It is a particularly relevant challenge to the Galatian believers, who were being tempted to see the fulfilment of the law of Christ in religious practices. How easily we can leave the way of love for the way of rules.

> *"For if anyone thinks himself to be something, when he is nothing, he deceives himself. But let each one examine his own work, and then he will have rejoicing in himself alone and not in another. For each shall bear his own load." (6:3-5)*

Here is the correct estimation of ourselves: nothing! NOTHING! The work of the cross is to bring proud, carnal, sinful man - to nothing, and then to impart Christ Himself. It is written in Job 26:7 that "God hangs the earth on nothing." Imagine for a moment that the earth were supported by steel girders and cables designed by the best engineers the world can offer. Reassuring? I rather think not!

Richard Wurmbrand describes how he was brought to nothing by years of solitary confinement and humiliation in a Communist prison camp in Romania. He was reduced to the point where he had nothing left; no dignity, no comfort, no hope of release, no wife or family and no friends. He was stripped naked, beaten and constantly lied to. When he had nothing to lose and nothing to offer God except himself, he found a peace and a presence that filled him with indescribable joy. In his famous sermon "The beauty of nothing" Wurmbrand describes taking communion with nothing. They had no bread and wine, not even poor substitutes and so celebrated communion with nothing. They held an imaginary cup to their mouths and ate imaginary bread. Though it may seem strange to others who have so much, yet his message is that when we are reduced to nothing, we enter through a door to find God Himself. Richard Wurmbrand's experience was extreme, but it was a similar path that many of God's greatest saints have trod. Moses lost his life of privilege in Egypt; he lost hope of leading a revolt when he had to flee from Egypt, and lived a life of insignificance and poverty in the harsh deserts of Arabia. When he had nothing left to offer God, God called him. Few people are called to such extreme experiences, but we are all called to learn from them.

Yes, we are of inestimable value to God, but our importance to Him does not lie in our abilities, or in the things that we contribute to His kingdom. Humility is a key manifestation of the fullness of the Spirit in the life of a man or woman. Verse 5 *"each one will bear his own load"* seems to contradict verse 2 *"bear one another's burdens"*, but while verse two refers to the need to help others, verse five refers to our watchfulness to fulfil our own ministry.

On that day, when we stand before the judgment seat of Christ, there will be no person who can help us - we will have to answer for ourselves. There is a reward for living this life in the Spirit and we receive that reward both in this life and the next. In this life we have the wonder of "rejoicing in ourselves alone" (Gal 6:4). By this phrase Paul is referring to the inner poise and joy that fills the hearts of those who live for others.

There is a moment in each person's experience, when our acts of devotion become dry and joyless. The only solution is to be refreshed in our life of loving and caring for others. We are not saved to be ornaments on God's shelf! We are to be well-used tools in His hands, and bear the loving marks of His workmanship in our lives.

## Galatians 6:6-10

*6 Let him who is taught the word share in all good things with him who teaches.*

*7 Do not be deceived, God is not mocked; for whatever a man sows, that he will also reap. 8 For he who sows to his flesh will of the flesh reap corruption, but he who sows to the Spirit will of the Spirit reap everlasting life. 9 And let us not grow weary while doing good, for in due season we shall reap if we do not lose heart. 10 Therefore, as we have opportunity, let us do good to all, especially to those who are of the household of faith.*

The joy that we reap in this life is a harvest from sowing to the Spirit. To sow to the Spirit is to flow in love and good works. If we live to merely fulfil our natural desires, then our spiritual life becomes corrupted, spoiled; including our awareness of God, our thirst for His word, our delight in His presence and ability to hear Him speak. We must not separate the practical from the spiritual. If only we can keep our hand to the plough, and not grow weary of well doing we will be richly rewarded in our spiritual lives. Many deep moves of God in churches and in individuals have dried up because there is no channelling of the blessing of God into action. The spiritual person will be looking for every opportunity to sow the seed of the word of God and excel in Christ-like actions. They will not just be dreaming but living out in flesh and blood the wonderful life of the Spirit.

This whole principle of sowing and reaping is a simple agricultural picture. The farmer sows, and knows therefore precisely what he will reap, but he will have to exercise patience as harvest may come months or even years later. This can be wonderfully encouraging but it also contains severe warnings. The warnings come for those who "sow to the flesh." They may claim that they have not received any negative effect from sin and selfish living. But the harvest is surely on its way, and when it comes, the seed sown will multiply and can bring its deadly reward in both mind and body.

The encouragement is for those who sow to the Spirit to persist without growing weary. When we lay down our lives in unselfish love, when we read our Bibles and spend time seeking to rest in His presence, we may not be aware of any immediate harvest. But keep going, for the harvest is on its way, and will bring multiplication. The key is not to grow weary. The greatest fruits come to those who patiently and persistently seek God's presence and receive His word.

---

Winston Churchill said:

*"Would you rise in the world? You must work while others amuse themselves. Are you desirous of a reputation for courage? You must risk your life. Would you be strong morally or physically? You must resist temptation. All this is paying in advance, that is, prospective finance. Observe the other side of the picture: the bad things are paid for afterwards."*

## *The apostle's passion*
## *Galatians 6:11-18*

> [11] See with what large letters I have written to you with my own hand! [12] As many as desire to make a good showing in the flesh, these would compel you to be circumcised, only that they may not suffer persecution for the cross of Christ. [13] For not even those who are circumcised keep the law, but they desire to have you circumcised that they may boast in your flesh. [14] But God forbid that I should boast except in the cross of our Lord Jesus Christ, by whom the world has been crucified to me, and I to the world. [15] For in Christ Jesus neither circumcision nor uncircumcision avails anything, but a new creation. [16] And as many as walk according to this rule, peace and mercy be upon them, and upon the Israel of God.
>
> [17] From now on let no one trouble me, for I bear in my body the marks of the Lord Jesus.
>
> [18] Brethren, the grace of our Lord Jesus Christ be with your spirit. Amen.

Paul closes this short letter with one of his most passionate appeals. This begins with the unusual fact that he had written at least part of this letter in his own rather clumsy handwriting (6:11). He had used rather large letters probably due to his poor eyesight. He had written this letter with personal interest and heartfelt passion. Paul refers to those who were legalistically promoting circumcision; seeking to win the Galatian believers in order to glory in the numbers they could win in support of their cause. Such details expose the emptiness of counting numbers in meetings, and trying to assess how many people have been blessed. Such practices reveal man-centred religion, detracting from the glory of God, and glorifying themselves. Those who hold this attitude seek popularity and praise from men and women. They run from the persecution and rejection which will often befall those who preach the cross (Gal 5:11; 6:12).

Paul's passion is the cross of Christ:

> *"God forbid that I should boast except in the cross of our Lord Jesus Christ, by whom the world has been crucified to me, and I to the world." (6:14)*

Paul is consumed with the cross and its effect on his life. It is Christ crucified that he had preached in Galatia (Gal 3:1). The cross had liberated him from sin (Gal 1:4), the curse of the law (Gal 3:13) and selfish worldly living (Gal 2:20; 5:24), and had renewed him and made into a new creature. By the cross Paul was dead to the world (Gal 6:14) and all its appeal to self realisation, through self indulgence and the pursuit of worldly success. It is for this message that he bears the marks of the cross in his body. No, there were no nail prints in his hands and feet, but there were many scars from the beatings, there were many visible signs of the sufferings and hardships he has gone through. He is not suggesting that his sufferings had any redemptive value, rather he is pointing to the effect of the cross in his life, enabling him to live with such carefree abandonment.

Truly the apostle Paul is an inspiration to us. He had received God's word deep into his being, and had allowed Jesus Christ to be Lord of his life. Paul was not an incarnation of God. He was still a man, capable of falling, capable of frustrating the grace of God. But by his yieldedness, he had allowed the power of the cross to burn through his whole being, making him a blazing witness to the power of redeeming love.

Paul's hope was not in a religious ritual, but in a powerful miracle of grace that had made him into a new person, a new creation. (6:15) This is his appeal, he is nothing in himself, but in and through the death of Jesus Christ, God had turned his whole life around, filling him with love and good works, flowing in the power of the Presence of God within him.

God can do it for anyone who is bold enough to take him at His word.

# Study Guide

# STUDY GUIDE A: GENERAL QUESTIONS

1. Who wrote this letter? Write down verses that teach you something personal about the author.

   - What was his former sinful life before he was a Christian?
   - How would you describe his relationship with the church of Galatia?
   - Do you find out anything about his health? Could this be his thorn in the flesh? (Gal 4:15; 6:11).

2. Who was he writing to? Write down verses that teach you something about the people of Galatia.

   - What was going wrong in Galatia?
   - Find out the names of some of the cities of Galatia where we know Paul preached in the book of Acts.
   - In the book of Acts, what miracles occurred in Galatia?

3. When was it written?

   - Try and place this letter in the book of Acts. Do you think it was written before or after the Council at Jerusalem mentioned in Acts 15? We may not be 100% certain about this, but form your own opinion.

4. What happened in Jerusalem and later in Antioch as described in Galatians chapter 2? Does anything surprise you about the way Paul speaks about the other apostles?

5. Why was Galatians written?

Which key verses highlight the problem in the church that Paul was trying to address?

6. The problem in Galatia was whether or not believers should be circumcised. This is not a problem in the church today. What are the problems of legalism that we find today?

<u>Additional questions for those wishing to study in more depth:</u>

7. The key words of this letter are:

- GRACE,
- LAW,
- FLESH,
- THE SPIRIT,
- JUSTIFICATION,
- CURSE,
- BLESSING.

    a. Find key verses for each of these.
    b. Write a definition for each word.
    c. Look up each word in a Bible dictionary and write down what you discover.
    d. Ask yourself if you agree with each definition. Note that some translations e.g. NIV does not translate the word "sarx" in the Greek as flesh, but paraphrases it. Do you agree with this paraphrase?

## Study Guide

8. The CROSS. The theme of Christ's sacrifice is mentioned seven times in this letter. The first one is in 1:4 "He gave Himself for our sins." See also: 2:20; 3:1; 3:13; 5:24; 6:12; 6:14. Meditate on all seven, and write a line indicating what each verse teaches you about the cross.

# STUDY GUIDE B: CHAPTER BY CHAPTER.

CHAPTER 1

1. (a) What claims does Paul make regarding his ministry and the gospel that he preaches? (See v 1)

(b) To what extent should we be able to make the same claims about our own ministry and the gospel that we preach? (Read also John 6:45).

2. Point out the verse that indicates the seriousness of preaching "another gospel."

3. In verses 13 and 14 Paul describes his life before his conversion. Make a list of the sins that characterized his life without Christ. Give special attention to his motives.

4. (a) Why is his conversion so wonderful?

(b) Do people in the world question or even mock the idea of Christian conversion?

(c) Describe the most wonderful things about your own conversion.

5. What was the importance of the time that Paul spent in Arabia?

6. What does this teach us about some of the things we should learn after our own conversion?

7. Why is it impossible to please men and be a servant of Christ at the same time? (v. 10)

## Study Guide

8. Paul says he was trying to "destroy faith" in v. 23. What things can destroy people's faith? How can we encourage people to build up their faith. And how can we build up our own faith?

9. What is the 'wonder' of the last words of chapter one?

10. Why do some translators have difficulty with verse 16? Some translate this "to reveal His son in me," while others say "reveal His son to me." The first is the literal translation. Does it make any difference?

*Take time to consider the wonder of His indwelling.*

## CHAPTER 2

1. (a) How does Paul describe the apostles in Jerusalem (see v.2, 6 & 9).

   (b) Why do you think he speaks of them like this?

   (c) Why do believers so easily cling to men in authority?

   (d) What is the snare of reputation? (Read also Philippians 2:7.)

2. (a) What is Peter's sin in verses 11-13?

   (b) Why was it so serious?

3. (a) What do you think of the way Paul dealt with the problem?

   (b) Why did he act so boldly?

4. Verse 18 speaks of things one must destroy to become a Christian. What do you think Paul means? Is there anything that you have had to destroy or eliminate from your life?

5. Verse 20 is the heart of this book and of the New Testament. Why is this so essential to Christian living?

6. At what point does a believer experience being 'crucified with Christ?'

7. (a) How are faith, grace and the cross linked together?

(b) Whose faith, whose grace and whose cross, is referred to? What does this teach you?

8. (a) What is the link between law, works and the flesh?

(b) How do these frustrate grace, faith and the cross?

9. (a) What was the issue at stake in Jerusalem (vv. 1-5) and Antioch (vv. 11-21).

(b) What issues do you think affect the churches today?

*Meditate on the wonder of being crucified with Christ.*

## CHAPTER 3

1. How do you think that Christ had been 'set forth as crucified' among the Galatians 3:1?

2. What is the key to receiving the Holy Spirit in verse 2?

3. What works might people be engaged in, who think they can receive the Spirit by the 'works of the law?'

4. (a) Paul says they "began in the Spirit". What does this tell you about the importance of receiving the Holy Spirit?

## Study Guide

(b) Is it the case that it sometimes takes God a long time to get a person to the starting line?

5. (a) Why do you think the law is linked with a curse?

(b) What is the link between Law, Curse and Flesh?

(c) What is the link between Promise, Blessing and the Gift of the Holy Spirit?

6. What is the blessing of Abraham (v. 14)?

7. In what way is the law our schoolmaster to bring us to Christ? (v. 23)

8. Verses 23 and 25 say that "faith came." What does this teach you about faith? (See also Rom. 10:17 and Eph. 2:8).

9. (a) Is everyone in the world a child of God? (verse 26).

(b) Does the Bible say that Abraham, Elijah and Moses were sons of God? Did they ever call God Father? What does this teach you about the difference between the Old and New Covenant?

(c) Comment on the impact of the words Jesus taught us to use in prayer: "OUR Father."

10. What is the baptism into Christ in verse 27?

11. What does it mean in verse 28, that there is neither Jew nor Greek, bond nor free, male nor female in Christ?

*Let the Holy Spirit fill you afresh now.*

## CHAPTER 4

In Hebrew culture a son was treated like a slave in the father's house, and was under tutors until the appointed time. When the boy came of age he was publicly declared to be the father's son. This is the cultural background to verses 1-9.

1. Being "under law" refers to the Old Testament. This is not only an ancient religious system, it explains something about the religious tendency of the human heart. What are the religious trappings and rituals that we might see around us today? Can you identify any in your own church?

2. "You desire to be in bondage" (v.9) and "you desire to be under law (v.21). Why do people desire to be under some legalistic form of religion?

3. (a) Paul was probably suffering from an eye problem. Comment on the way he was received by the Galatian believers (v.15).

   (b) Is it unusual that God should use a disabled man with such an illness?

   (c) What was Paul's attitude to his weakness? (See 1 Corinthians 2:4-5 and 2 Corinthians 12:7-11).

   (d) How does this accord with the commonly held view that apostles are supermen? What does it teach you about life in the Spirit?

4. God has sent His Spirit to witness in our hearts that we are children and heirs of God (vv. 6-7). What is our inheritance?

5. What is the 'travail in birth' referring to in verse 19?

6. Who is the 'mother of all' that are born from above (v. 26)?

7. (a) What is the conflict between the 'child of the flesh' and the 'child of the Spirit' referred to in verse 29?

(b) What then is this conflict? Denominations? Youth v age? Jew v Gentile?

(c) How do we cast out the 'bondwoman and her son' (v.30)? What do they represent in our experience?

*Let the wonder and joy of Sonship fill your heart.*


## CHAPTER 5

1. We are either walking in the Spirit or in the flesh. There is no middle ground. How is this truth expressed in verses 2-5 and 16-17?

2. Comment on the following keys to life in the Spirit:

(a) Verse 1. "Stand fast" on what ground? And against whom or what?

(b) Verse 5. "We through the Spirit wait." How do we learn to wait? Why is this so against the flesh?

(c) Verse 7. "You ran well." What makes us run?

(d) Verse 16. "Walk." What does this image teach us about spiritual life? Reflect on how babies and adults walk, and the lessons we can learn from this.

3. "Faith working through love." (v6) Why must love always be the motive for true faith? Think of things that Jesus did that required great love and faith, such as washing the disciples' feet.

4. "By love serve one another" (v. 13) and "you shall love your neighbour as yourself" (v. 14). Why are the cross and loving behaviour so closely linked?

5. The works of the flesh (v. 19) describe the heart of sinful people. Do the law and unregenerate men and women go 'hand in hand?'

6. Does the fruit of the Spirit work by law? If not, why not?

7. How are we to bear the fruit of the Spirit?

8. How do we crucify the flesh with its lusts? (v. 24).

9. What are the passions and desires of the flesh? Are they all sinful in themselves? When does normal appetite become a dangerous lust?

*Reflect on the joy of Christian living in the Spirit.*

## CHAPTER 6

1. Verse one describes the manner of church discipline for someone who has fallen into sin.

   (a) What does it mean to be overtaken in any trespass?

   (b) What does it mean to "restore" a person?

   (c) There are several key attitudes needed in the heart of someone who is to counsel a person who has fallen from grace. What are they?

   (d) How do these attitudes relate to the previous chapter?

   (e) How can we help bear the burden of one who has fallen?

## Study Guide

2. What is the Law of Christ (v. 2)?

3. Verse 5 speaks of a different burden that no one can help us to bear. What is this burden?

4. (a) Why is the assessment of ourselves (v. 3) so important if we are to walk in the Spirit?

   (b) What is a correct estimation of ourselves?

5. (a) How do we sow to the Spirit? Give examples from this chapter and other scriptures.

   (b) How do we sow to the flesh?

6. "A good showing in the flesh" (v. 12).

   (a) How do individuals do this?

   (b) How do churches do this?

7. (a) What does he mean by "the world" in v. 14?

   (b) What is the key to being free from the world and its temptations?

8. What is the "rule" in v. 16?

9. What are the marks that Paul bore in his body (v. 17)? How might we bear such marks in our lives?

*We enter into the benefits of the cross by a definite act of repentance and faith. Are you claiming the power of the cross to overcome the enemies of spiritual life? Receive the wondrous grace of God that sets you free.*

Made in the USA
Charleston, SC
05 April 2015